THE ART OF
KIPPER
READING

DECODING POWERFUL MESSAGES

ALEXANDRE MUSRUCK

REDFeather™
MIND | BODY | SPIRIT

4880 Lower Valley Road, Atglen, PA 19310

Designed by Danielle D. Farmer
Cover design by Ashley Millhouse
Type set in Engravers MT/Minion Pro

ISBN: 978-0-7643-5901-9
Printed in China

Published by Red Feather Mind, Body, Spirit
An imprint of Schiffer Publishing, Ltd.
4880 Lower Valley Road
Atglen, PA 19310
Phone: (610) 593-1777; Fax: (610) 593-2002
E-mail: Info@schifferbooks.com
Web: www.redfeathermbs.com

For our complete selection of fine books on this and related subjects, please visit our website at www.schifferbooks.com. You may also write for a free catalog.

Schiffer Publishing's titles are available at special discounts for bulk purchases for sales promotions or premiums. Special editions, including personalized covers, corporate imprints, and excerpts, can be created in large quantities for special needs. For more information, contact the publisher.

We are always looking for people to write books on new and related subjects. If you have an idea for a book, please contact us at proposals@schifferbooks.com.

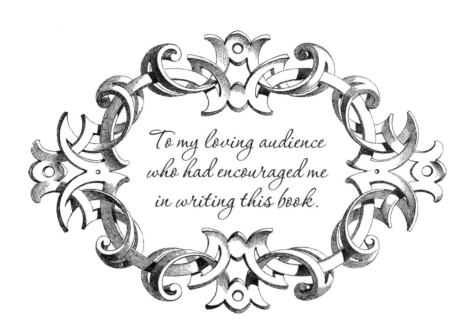

To my loving audience
who had encouraged me
in writing this book.

CONTENTS

ABOUT THE KIPPER CARDS

Alexandre Musruck Kipper Oracle Cards

A French Adaptation of the
Original German Kipperkarten

THE MAIN
CHARACTERS

$\mathcal{I}$n 1890, in Germany, appeared the *Kipper Fortune-Telling Cards*, a deck that clearly reflects the founding period, an era in which Germany was in the economic boom. The illustration clearly shows that the deck is from Bavaria, a state in the southeast of Germany. The deck, like Lenormand, bears the name of famous fortune teller Madame Susanne Kipper, but here again there is no evidence that it was created by her or simply a marketing strategy. In 1920, the publishing right went to the company FX Schmid and in 1996 on to the Altenburger Spielkartenfabrik.

There is voice that
doesn't use words. Listen.

—RUMI

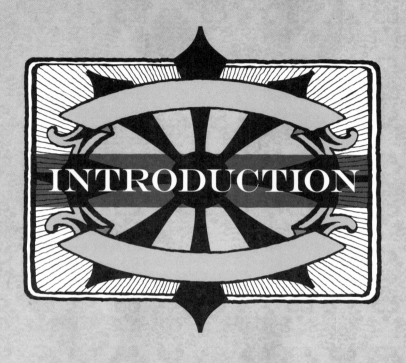

INTRODUCTION

$\mathcal{W}$elcome in the Mysterious World of Kipperkarten (Kipper cards). My name is Alexandre Musruck, and I've been reading cards for the last 23 years. I started at a very young age (11 years old) using simple playing cards. I first saw Tarot in the James Bond movie *Live and Let Die*, where Solitaire, a psychic in the employ of Dr. Kananga, describes the journey of Bond as he travels to New York by plane, via the use of the cards. This movie had a real impact upon me and triggered my interest. In my book *The Art of Lenormand Reading*, I talk about how the Petit Lenormand came to me, and how its entrance changed my life in an amazing way. This experience opened up my curiosity to other methods of cartomancy, and I found the Kipperkarten, a strange deck from Germany.

I found the way of reading the Kipper very similar to the Lenormand, but instead of simple symbol as an anchor, a tree, or a ring, I found a myriad of personage and events: the good lady, a rich girl, the Main Female, a marriage, and a meeting, to name some. With this deck, again, I discovered a sense of familiarity as these persons and events reminded me of my playing cards: the queen of clubs, 8 of clubs, queen of hearts, ace of clubs, and 10 of hearts. Lenormand had awakened a great interest in the United States, and people started to look for old divination systems from Europe. They were intrigued by the Kipperkarten, a close sister to Lenormand. Unfortunately, there was little information about divining with this fabulous deck, and nearly all the resources available were written in German, the native language of the Kipperkarten. Many contacted me as they knew about my working with the Kipper for several years and told me about their search for a book about that type of deck. With the success of my first Lenormand book and all the amazing feedback I received, I thought that I would provide such a book since I had been using it in my private practice with my clients.

What I love about the Kipper is that their messages are to the point; they can tell you everything about your love life, what your lover is thinking, how this morning's meeting will go, if you can trust "John," and everything you need to know about your life in general. My wish is that this book becomes your key to unlock the wisdom of the Kipper cards; it's an easy-to-read book with relatively simple text, making it accessible to everyone. I've put all my heart, time, and expertise in these pages and hope you will feel the passion I have for card reading.

With all my love,

ALEXANDRE MUSRUCK

$\mathcal{L}$et's take a moment to look at each card and study them carefully; it's important that you familiarize yourself with the cards. These cards will make you travel between worlds through their wisdom. The 36 cards are in numerical order:

THE KIPPER DECK

No. 1	Main Male	No. 19	A Funeral
No. 2	Main Female	No. 20	The House
No. 3	Marriage	No. 21	The Living Room
No. 4	A Meeting	No. 22	A Military
No. 5	The Good Lord	No. 23	The Court
No. 6	The Good Lady	No. 24	The Thievery
No. 7	A Pleasant Letter	No. 25	High Honours
No. 8	False Person	No. 26	Big Luck
No. 9	A Change	No. 27	Unexpected Money
No. 10	A Journey	No. 28	Expectation
No. 11	Lot of Money	No. 29	The Prison
No. 12	A Rich Girl	No. 30	Legal Matters
No. 13	A Rich Man	No. 31	Short Illness
No. 14	Sad News	No. 32	Grief and Sorrow
No. 15	Success in Love	No. 33	Murky Thoughts
No. 16	His Thoughts	No. 34	Occupation
No. 17	A Gift	No. 35	A Long Road
No. 18	Small Child	No. 36	Hope, Big Water

I broke the deck into categories to help you understand their core essence: 9 cards representing people (who play major or minor roles in a reading) are:

The Main Male	No. 1	**A Rich Girl**	No. 12
The Main Female	No. 2	**A Rich Man**	No. 13
The Good Lord	No. 5	**Small Child**	No. 18
The Good Lady	No. 6	**A Military**	No. 22
False Person	No. 8		

These people can also represent people in your family circle and can provide valuable information on their influence, for instance:

The Good Lord—No. 5
Father, father-in-law, grandfather, an uncle, or an ex-husband

The Good Lady—No. 6
Mother, mother-in-law, grandmother, an aunt, or an ex-wife

A Rich Girl—No. 12
Sister, daughter, sister-in-law, a daughter-in-law, a niece, or any young female relative

A Rich Man—No. 13
Son, brother, brother-in-law, son-in-law, a nephew, or any young male relative

Small Child—No. 18
Your child, your baby, or a Small Child in the family

Some cards can point out particular events and situations, and the cards around them can give valuable information on the issues. The cards are:

Marriage	No. 3	**A Journey**	No. 10
A Meeting	No. 4	**Lot of Money**	No. 11
A Pleasant Letter	No. 7	**Success in Love**	No. 15
A Change	No. 9	**A Funeral**	No. 19

The Thievery	No. 24	**Expectation**	No. 28
High Honours	No. 25	**Legal Matters**	No. 30
Big Luck	No. 26	**Short Illness**	No. 31
Unexpected Money	No. 27		

When you want to look into a particular event and see how things will go, just locate the card in the spread and read the cards around it. In the chapter concerning direction, I explain the proper way to interpret a card.

The following cards are attached to objects and places; the cards around them affect the mood and energy of these cards. They are:

A Journey	No. 10	**The Court**	No. 23
A Pleasant Letter	No. 7	**The Prison**	No. 29
A Gift	No. 17	**A Long Road**	No. 35
The House	No. 20	**Hope, Big Water**	No. 36
The Living Room	No. 21		

These cards are handy particularly if you are looking for a missing object; the cards can point out particular places, for instance. The Prison card could say the object is behind a lot of stuff or blocked somewhere between things; with the Living Room card, it indicates this area of the house and with travel—for sure, it has been lost away from home.

Certain cards are a warning against danger and really get your attention. Remember that the course of events can always be modified if you choose to act accordingly. Remember that an oracle is empowering rather than fatalistic. The cards of warning are:

False Person	No. 8	**The Thievery**	No. 24
Small Child	No. 18	**Grief and Sorrow**	No. 32
(refers to naivety)		**Murky Thoughts**	No. 33
A Funeral	No. 19		

This final group of cards show profession, aligning to the energy of the cards. They are:

Lot of Money (Money win)—No. 11
Investors, stock exchange, casino worker, financier

A Rich Girl—No. 12
Bank employee, accountant, moneylender

A Rich Man—No. 13
Bank employee, accountant, moneylender

A Military—No. 22
All professions that require a uniform: doctor, policeman, nurse, etc.

High Honours—No. 25
Teacher, manager, minister, politician, person of great position

Occupation—No. 34
This is the job card, and surrounding cards will tell what kind of work is involved; refer to the card combinations for more details

BEFORE WE

START

BUY YOURSELF A DECK

Choosing a deck is the very first step. The original Kipperkarten is still available, so you can choose the original or the companion deck for this book.

DIRECTION

In German cartomancy, direction is very important; the way your significators card no. 1 or no. 2 is looking or facing is key. This will define the past and the future, the lucky or unlucky events that the seeker will go through.

INTENTION

Before framing your question, you must decide what you want the cards to tell you: Is it an advice? Describe the personality of someone or simply a prediction you want from the cards. Do not read the Kipper as the Tarot; they are different systems. Whatever you ask the cards, they will tell you; they are never wrong—it's the interpretation that sometimes is wrong.

FRAME YOUR QUESTION

Clear question = Clear answer! Formulate your question as clearly as possible. Visualize it in your head, speak it aloud, or even write it down on paper, and pay extra attention to the context and direction as the meaning of the cards and its messages will change.

JOURNALING

Keeping a record of your reading is very useful. You can keep track on how a certain card had a particular meaning in a particular situation. I really enjoy walking through my old notebooks to see how the reading of the cards has worked out; it is a way of learning. Let me tell you that my old journals have given birth to this book.

PRACTICE MAKES PERFECT

The more you practice, the more you will gain experience. It's like working a muscle—the more you use it, the stronger it becomes. You can practice on everything, from the issue of a national election to the sex of your neighbor's upcoming baby. This will build your confidence as a card reader.

THE

KIPPER DECK

ANATOMY

$\mathcal{L}$et's have a close look at the structure of the Kipper cards; each card has a central scene, and the meaning is always modified by the surrounding cards. The cards are read like pictograms, and combining their meaning results in a phrase, telling a story.

Each card has different meaning, and again, the meaning will depend on the context of your question and direction of the cards; context and direction are key in reading the Kipper! The way the cards face each other will alter their meaning and highly influence your read. I will explain more about this further in the chapter dedicated to Direction. Before that, let's take a look at the actors of the game: the Signifiers!

Card Number

24

The Thievery

Image of
a character,
a scene,
or event

Card Title

THE

SIGNIFIERS, SIGNIFICATORS, PERSON CARDS, AND

MAIN CHARACTERS

The two cards below will represent the querent depending on their sex; if a man comes to you for a reading, he will be represented by card 1 (the Main Male), and the Main Female (card 2) can represent his wife or a significant woman in his life. Inversely, for a woman who comes for a reading, she would be represented by card 2 (the Main Female), and the Main Male (card 1) would represent her husband or a significant man in her life.

THE SIGNIFIERS OR MAIN CHARACTERS

MAN
MALE QUERENT

WOMAN
WOMAN QUERENT

In Kipper, the Main Male and Main Female direction (see the diagram) is very important. This will tell you if their relation is harmonious or not; the direction they look at each other will define their past and future. The diagram that follows shows a different story when the main characters face each other, and another one when they are back to back.

DISHARMONIOUS RELATIONSHIP

DIRECTION
FACING LEFT

DIRECTION
FACING RIGHT

The Main Male is looking in this direction

The Main Female is looking in this direction

+

The characters are back to back—a sign of a position of argument

HARMONIOUS RELATIONSHIP

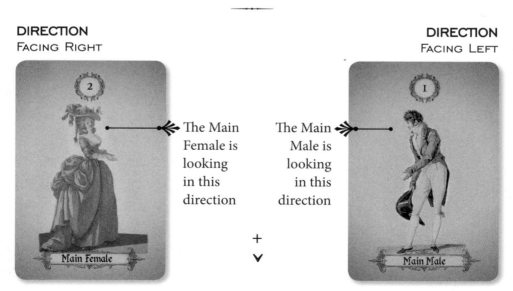

DIRECTION
FACING RIGHT

DIRECTION
FACING LEFT

The Main Female is looking in this direction

The Main Male is looking in this direction

+

The characters are face to face—a sign of harmonious interaction

DIRECTION

$\mathcal{T}$his is the crucial part of the Kipper system; everything lies here. You can understand and get the card meaning engraved in your brain, but if Direction is not understood, your reading will not be accurate, and you may as well throw your cards in the trash. I will use images and diagrams to teach the Direction; remember that we are using a German system of cartomancy, and we should respect the rules of this school/tradition.

In the French cartomancy tradition, everything that is on the left-hand side is the past, and everything that is on the right-hand side is the future— wherever the person's card is facing to the right or left. But with Kipper cards, the position of the seeker is key! If your person's card faces left, everything on the left side is his future, and everything at his back, where his eyes are not looking, is the past. Everything that appears on top of the Significator card is things that are on his thoughts, things that have not materialized yet, and everything that is under him is things that he has mastered and has control over. I found that this position does define the quality and personality of the seeker, a precious piece of information that can help you understand why things are that way.

As mentioned before, when one of the main characters faces a card, the meaning is different from when this same card faces away. Direction is applied not only to the Main Characters card No. 1 and No. 2, but to any third parties you want to have information about. For instance, if you would like to look at your mother's impact on the reading, you will look at The Good Lady and read the cards around her; same for a sister, where you would choose A Rich Girl instead to represent her (refer to the chart concerning family members). In the card-meaning section, I will provide all the possible combinations of the whole deck in the Left, Right, Top, and Bottom positions, providing an important, handy amount of information to help you gain clarity and precision in your reading. The following diagram explains what the four position are, what they mean, and how they affect the interpretation of the card layout.

WHEN THE CHARACTERS
FACE LEFT

- What is on the mind
- What is unknown
- What is important at the moment

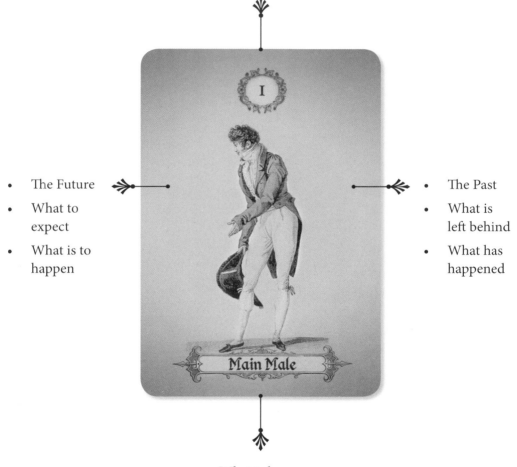

- The Future
- What to expect
- What is to happen

- The Past
- What is left behind
- What has happened

- What is known
- What is achieved
- What is mastered

WHEN THE CHARACTERS FACE RIGHT

- What is on the mind
- What is unknown
- What is important at the moment

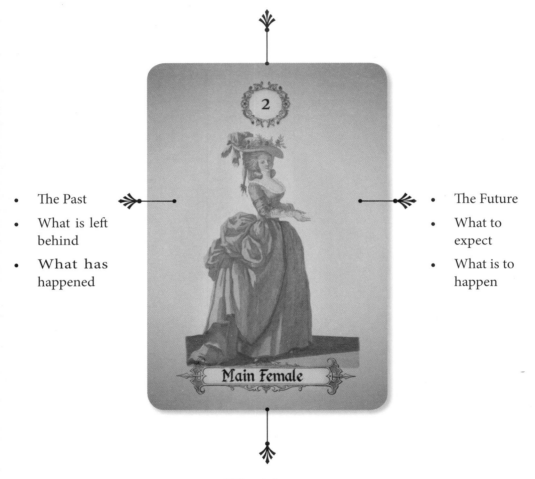

- The Past
- What is left behind
- **What has happened**

- The Future
- What to expect
- What is to happen

- What is known
- What is achieved
- What is mastered

So keep in mind that the way you would read Kipper is by using the method of directionality.

THE 36 CARD

MEANINGS

*B*efore jumping into the card meanings, let me give you a brief introduction to what we are going to study and talk about. Like in my book *The Art of Lenormand Reading: Decoding the Powerful Messages Conveyed by the Lenormand Oracle*, I've arranged the meaning section in a way that you access directly to the core meaning for each card, and you can run through the book whenever you feel stuck with a card. I've charted the meaning so that you can easily find it.

In each card section, you will find:

Keywords: The basic keywords

Meaning of the card: The core meaning of the card

Mantra: A positive mantra that you can use in this situation

Influence: If the card is positive, negative, or neutral

Direction: In what direction is the card facing

Quick answer: A Yes, No, or Maybe answer

Topic card: The area that the card rules

Card combination: The interaction of two cards and their meanings, plus a left, right, top, and bottom position for each of the person's card, i.e.,

Main Male—No. 1

Main Female—No. 2

The Good Lord—No. 5

The Good Lady—No. 6

False Person—No. 8

A Rich Girl—No. 12

A Rich Man—No. 13

Small Child—No. 18

A Military—No. 22

Choose the meaning that best suits the context of your question, as not all combos listed here will be applicable. With time and experience you will build your own sets of meaning and add to it gradually; till then, my combos will help you get started.

I've also added real stories related to readings that I've performed for my clients where the cards have been extremely clear, precise, and so accurate. This part I think will help you see how the cards can interact and provide amazing readings.

NOTE

I want to thank my clients who have kindly accepted that I put their stories in my book; I've changed their names so that confidentiality is respected. One of my rules is that what happens between me and my clients stays between us; they choose if they want to sharev what they've experienced during a reading with others.

NO. 1
MAIN MALE

Keywords

Male Questioner, Partner, Husband

*T*he Main Male card represents the male asking for the reading; the cards around him will have a direct impact upon him. If it is the case that it's a woman asking for a reading, the Main Male protagonist may represent a husband, a partner, or any significant man in her life.

When you are doing your reading, especially the Grand Tableau (see chapter twelve), it is important to locate this card and look closely at the cards surrounding it: Those on his left are his future; those on his right reveal the past; those above him are things that are on his mind, his intention, his thoughts, and his plans; and finally those below are things he has achieved; these can also reveal his qualities as well as his imperfection.

Mantra: I am the master of my life.

Influence: Neutral

Direction: Facing left

Quick answer: Maybe

Topic card: All

When the following appear on the LEFT of
No. 1—Main Male

When the following appear on the LEFT of
No. 1—Main Male

The Future

No. 2 — **Main Female:** Harmonious relationship, meeting a significant woman, future partner to come, a positive start, a time of sharing and discovery.

No. 3 — **Marriage:** Happily married man, the querent is looking forward to a commitment, a partnership is on its way, a positive deal or contract.

No. 4 — **A Meeting:** An appointment, a social gathering, an event, meeting a group.

No. 5 — **The Good Lord:** Dealing with an older man, a supportive friend, a father.

No. 6 — **The Good Lady:** Dealing with an older woman, supportive female friend.

No. 7 — **A Pleasant Letter:** Good news, news to come, positive correspondence, positive phone calls.

No. 8 — **False Person:** Enemy, rival, cunning dangerous person, pay attention!

No. 9 — **A Change:** A change is imminent, the Main Male will move or relocate, a change in the plan will succeed.

No. 10 — **A Journey:** A change in the plan will succeed, a positive trip, embarking for a journey.

No. 11 — **Lot of Money:** Financial stability, money comes in, wealth and abundance, luxury.

No. 12 — **A Rich Girl:** Interaction with a daughter, a sister, or any young female relative; closeness with a young female, a young lover.

No. 13 — **A Rich Man:** Interaction with a son, a brother, or any young male relative; closeness with a young male, a young lover.

No. 14 — **Sad News:** Receiving negative or sad news, a depressed mood, dealing with some bad news.

No. 15 — **Success in Love:** The Main Male falls in love, love affair, a happy and positive love life.

No. 16 — **His Thoughts:** The seeker is preoccupied, very thoughtful, a lot going on in his mind.

No. 17 — **A Gift:** External circumstances bring joy, a gift, a pleasant visit.

No. 18 — **Small Child:** A new beginning, a pregnancy, the querent is innocent.

No. 19 — **A Funeral:** An ending, a separation, assisting a funeral.

No. 20 — **The House:** Buying a property, a cozy man, family house.

No. 21 — **The Living Room:** The querent feels at home, the querent's personal space.

No. 22 — **A Military:** Official matters are on the agenda, encountering someone wearing a uniform.

No. 23 — **The Court:** A final decision, justice triumphs, official matter will be regulated.

No. 24 — **The Thievery:** Recovering a lost object, the thief is caught.

No. 25 — **High Honours:** The querent is successful, he receives recognition, a promotion may be on the horizon.

No. 26 — **Big Luck:** The querent is lucky, he can expect happy outcome and lot of success in his ventures.

No. 27 — **Unexpected Money:** A windfall, contracts well negotiated are now paying off, unexpected happy surprise.

No. 28 — **Expectation:** The querent is patient and has strong desires; the next card will say what kind of expectation he has.

No. 29 — **The Prison:** The querent is restricted in his actions, loneliness, locked away, correctional facility, standstill, stagnation.

No. 30 — **Legal Matters:** Seeing a lawyer, seeking expertise, dealing with legal matters.

No. 31 — **Short Illness:** Weak health condition, fever, small infection, light depression, need to rest, need to sleep.

No. 32 — **Grief and Sorrow:** A difficult time to come, problems and difficulties pile up in front of you. A pattern, a depression, addiction.

No. 33 — **Murky Thoughts:** A negative mood, lost in fear, drama queen, negative thinking.

No. 34 — **Occupation:** Hardworking, motivated, ambitious man, a job offer.

No. 35 — **A Long Road:** Traveling to a distant destination, have patience because things will not happen now.

No. 36— **Hope, Big Water:** Traveling abroad, crossing waters; event will happen in a foreign land; feeling hopeful, an intuitive.

When the following appear on the RIGHT of
No. 1—Main Male

The Past

No. 2 — **Main Female:** Distance between lovers, a risk of separation, the male querent had turned the page.

No. 3 — **Marriage:** Major problems in the partnership, the querent is single, he has been through a breakup, letting go of a relationship.

No. 4 — **A Meeting:** A past meeting, an event had taken place, taking distance from a group of people, leaving a meet-up.

No. 5 — **The Good Lord:** Turning away from an elder person, contact with an elder is difficult, father/son relationship issue.

No. 6 — **The Good Lady:** Turning away from an elder person, contact with an elder is difficult, mother/daughter relationship issue.

No. 7 — **A Pleasant Letter:** A message sent, past communication, past conversation.

No. 8 — **False Person:** Away from enemy, rival, and cunning; dangerous person from the past.

No. 9 — **A Change:** A recent change, recent move or relocation, surrounding cards will predict what kind of change is to happen.

No. 10 — **A Journey:** The querent had left a person, place, or situation; a recent travel; a planned trip didn't turn out the way it was hoped.

No. 11 — **Lot of Money:** Financial crisis, money goes, the querent does not see this opportunity, the querent turns back to a positive transaction.

No. 12 — **A Rich Girl:** Dispute with a daughter, a sister, or any young female relative. Turning away a young female, a generation gap.

No. 13 — **A Rich Man:** Dispute with a son, a brother, or any young male relative. Turning away a young male, a generation gap.

No. 14 — **Sad News:** Negative or sad news from the past, depression is over, letting go of sadness.

No. 15 — **Success in Love:** The Main Male was in love. A love affair is over, a positive relationship from the past.

No. 16 — **His Thoughts:** The seeker is no longer preoccupied; he has been through a period of reflection, and now the solution had been found.

No. 17 — **A Gift:** External circumstances have brought joy, the querent was visited, a gift was received.

No. 18 — **Small Child:** Abortion, a miscarriage. Children are a source of worry, not the right time for a new beginning.

No. 19 — **A Funeral:** The querent lost someone, something is now buried. A breaking free, coming through a transformation, coming through grief.

No. 20 — **The House:** Selling a property. The Main Male leaves the safety of his walls.

No. 21 — **The Living Room:** Not feeling at home, feeling rejected, leaving the comfort behind.

No. 22 — **A Military:** Official matters are over, leaving the uniform.

No. 23 — **The Court:** Official matter is regulated; the Main Male was wrong or guilty.

No. 24 — **The Thievery:** Something or someone is taken away. The thief escaped.

No. 25 — **High Honours:** A temporary acknowledgment, past acknowledgment.

No. 26 — **Big Luck:** Unlucky situation, unfaithful outcome, a failure.

No. 27 — **Unexpected Money:** Bankruptcy, unprofitable transaction, transaction at a loss, in dire straits.

No. 28 — **Expectation:** Patience is over, the Main Male has met a middle-aged woman.

No. 29 — **The Prison:** Restrictions are over, end of a standstill and stagnation.

No. 30 — **Legal Matters:** The Main Male feels wronged; the lawyer is not in favor of the Main Male.

No. 31 — **Short Illness:** Recovery from a short illness, health impairment.

No. 32 — **Grief and Sorrow:** Gone through difficult time, out of a depression, healing from addiction.

No. 33 — **Murky Thoughts:** Disenchantment, leaving the drama queen behind.

No. 34 — **Occupation:** Distancing oneself from work, or has been working hard lately.

No. 35 — **A Long Road:** Was away to a distant destination, has shown a lot of patience or was running out of patience.

No. 36 — **Hope, Big Water:** The Main Male lost hope, coming from abroad in a foreign land, feeling hopeful, a dream had manifested into reality.

When the following appear on the TOP of (above)
No. 1—Main Male

On the Mind

No. 2 —   **Main Female:** He is thinking of a particular woman—his spouse, his partner, a significant woman in his life.

No. 3 —   **Marriage:** The Main Male dreams of a harmonious relationship, thinking about a future partnership or deal.

No. 4 —   **A Meeting:** Thinking of an appointment, a social gathering, an event, meeting a group.

No. 5 —   **The Good Lord:** Thinking of an older man, a supportive friend, a father, an elder male.

No. 6 —   **The Good Lady:** Thinking of an older woman, a supportive female friend, an elder female.

No. 7 —   **A Pleasant Letter:** The querent longs for better communication, thinking of a message or a correspondence.

No. 8 —   **False Person:** Thinking of an enemy, a rival; a cunning, dangerous person. Mind manipulation.

No. 9 —   **A Change:** Thinking of a change, the Main Male thinks of a move or a relocation, thinking, wishing, or hoping for a change.

No. 10 —   **A Journey:** Thinking of a planned change, of a trip. Longing for a particular destination.

No. 11 —   **Lot of Money:** The querent thinks of his financial stability, constantly thinking of his finances; money is very important for the querent.

No. 12 —   **A Rich Girl:** Thinking of a daughter, a sister, or any young female relative; thinking of a young lover.

No. 13 —   **A Rich Man:** Thinking of a son, a brother, or any young male relative; thinking of a young lover.

No. 14 —   **Sad News:** Sorrowful thoughts, fear of bad news, negative thoughts.

No. 15 —   **Success in Love:** Thinking of success, thinking of his love life.

No. 16 —   **His Thoughts:** The seeker is thinking a lot right now.

No. 17 —   **A Gift:** Thinking of a gift, thoughts of a pleasant visit.

No. 18 —   **Small Child:** Thinking of a new beginning, innocent thoughts, naive thoughts, planning something new, thinking of a baby.

No. 19 — **A Funeral:** Thinking of an ending, of a separation; thinking of a funeral.

No. 20 — **The House:** Thinking of a property, of constructing something. Thinking of the family.

No. 21 — **The Living Room:** Thinking of his private life, thinking of things going on around the house.

No. 22 — **A Military:** A feeling of being controlled, thinking of a strategy, making up a battle plan.

No. 23 — **The Court:** Thinking of a legal issue, thinking about an important decision, thinking of a deadline.

No. 24 — **The Thievery:** Thinking of a lost object, reviewing a loss; the Main Male thinks about taking something away.

No. 25 — **High Honours:** The querent thinks about studying; he is intelligent and aware of his talents and capacities.

No. 26 — **Big Luck:** The querent thinks of his luck, of the various doors opening before him.

No. 27 — **Unexpected Money:** The querent thinks of a contract, of a lucrative deal. He may also be worried by his finances at the moment.

No. 28 — **Expectation:** Thinking about a middle-aged woman, thinking of one's goal and motives, thinking about the future of things.

No. 29 — **The Prison:** The querent is thinking about his loneliness, dreaming of freedom. Closed-minded.

No. 30 — **Legal Matters:** Considering the help of a lawyer, considering legal disputes.

No. 31 — **Short Illness:** Thinking about his weak health condition, insomnia; the querent should uplift his thoughts in this situation.

No. 32 — **Grief and Sorrow:** Thinking of a difficult time to come, problems and difficulties are piling up, facing a depression or even an addiction.

No. 33 — **Murky Thoughts:** Negative mood, lost in fear, drama queen, negative thinking.

No. 34 — **Occupation:** Preoccupied by his work, the querent's job involved a lot of his logic and intelligence.

No. 35 — **A Long Road:** Thinking of a distant destination, the querent plans things in advance.

No. 36 — **Hope, Big Water:** Fascinated by foreign culture; a need to ground himself.

When the following appear at the BOTTOM of
No. 1—Main Male

Has Achieved

No. 2 — **Main Female:** The Main Male has a partner, a spouse; he has someone significant in his life.

No. 3 — **Marriage:** The Main Male is a happily married man, is in a committed relationship/partnership, achieved positive deals and contracts.

No. 4 — **A Meeting:** Is a very social person, involved in events, gatherings, and get-togethers.

No. 5 — **The Good Lord:** Is a good person, supportive of his friends, a good father.

No. 6 — **The Good Lady:** Is a good person, supportive of her friends, a good mother.

No. 7 — **A Pleasant Letter:** Has a pleasant personality, communicates a lot with others, and is often the bearer of good news.

No. 8 — **False Person:** The querent may be sabotaging himself; he is his own rival. A cunning personality; he needs to change the way he behaves in life.

No. 9 — **A Change:** He is a changed man; has been through a lot lately.

No. 10 — **A Journey:** Our querent is a kind of gypsy, always on the road; his work may involve travel (e.g., a truck driver).

No. 11 — **Lot of Money:** Has a financial stability, he sits on money, he may be someone who controls every penny spent.

No. 12 — **A Rich Girl:** Is close to his daughter, sister, or any young female relative. Acting like a spoiled child as well.

No. 13 — **A Rich Man:** Is close to his son, brother, or any young male relative. Acting like a spoiled child as well.

No. 14 — **Sad News:** Has a displeasing personality, complains about everything, and is often the bearer of bad news.

No. 15 — **Success in Love:** The Main Male is a loyal partner, tied to his intention, respectful of his relationship; can be trusted at 100%.

No. 16 — **His Thoughts:** Is more of an action man than someone who plan things in advance; he is more logical than practical.

No. 17 — **A Gift:** Loves to give and receive, with a surprising personality and known to be a gift to others.

No. 18 — **Small Child:** Has achieved a new beginning, is a father to come, can also be someone with a naive personality.

No. 19 — **A Funeral:** Closely experienced an ending, a separation, or death.

No. 20 — **The House:** Is the owner of his property, a cozy man; he is a family man, tied to family values.

No. 21 — **The Living Room:** Is a secretive man, protecting his privacy and intimacy, very attached to his home and family.

No. 22 — **A Military:** Is someone who wears a uniform; he likes discipline and order, ruling his life and business with righteousness.

No. 23 — **The Court:** High minded, the querent is someone who has principles; he always honors deadlines.

No. 24 — **The Thievery:** The querent is someone who takes things away; he tends to steal from other people and snatches what he wants.

No. 25 — **High Honours:** The querent is acknowledged, enjoying a good reputation, and is respected as a leader.

No. 26 — **Big Luck:** The querent is a lucky man; he acknowledges it and uses his luck in every other venture.

No. 27 — **Unexpected Money:** Our querent is someone who deals well with his contract, and his income is constantly increasing.

No. 28 — **Expectation:** Patience is a virtue for our querent; he is always alert, paying attention to what is on the horizon.

No. 29 — **The Prison:** The querent is solitary; he may be sabotaging himself.

No. 30 — **Legal Matters:** The querent is avid for counsel and advice and uses his wisdom to restore peace and happiness.

No. 31 — **Short Illness:** He is an insomniac and does not enjoy a good health. He may have sexual problems.

No. 32 —**Grief and Sorrow:** The querent is a depressive, addicted person.

No. 33 — **Murky Thoughts:** Always sees the glass half empty, likes to keep himself worrying in dark thoughts.

No. 34 — **Occupation:** Hardworking, motivated, ambitious man.

No. 35 — **A Long Road:** He is patient in his action and waits for the perfect time to act.

No. 36 — **Hope, Big Water:** The querent is a gifted one; he may have psychic abilities or any kind of artistic talent.

*I am neither of the East nor of the West,
no boundaries exist with my breast.*

—RUMI

NO. 2
MAIN FEMALE

Keywords
Female Questioner, Partner, Wife

*T*he Main Female card represents the female asking for the reading; the cards around her will have a direct impact upon her life. In case it's a man asking for a reading, the Main Female may represent his wife, partner, or any significant woman in his life.

When you are doing your reading, especially the Grand Tableau, it is important to locate this card and look closely at the cards surrounding it: Those on her left are her past; those on her right reveal the future; those above her are things that are on her mind, her intention, her thoughts, and her plans; and finally those below are things she has achieved and can also reveal her qualities as well as her imperfections.

Mantra: I am the master of my life.

Influence: Neutral

Direction: Facing right

Quick answer: Maybe

Topic card: All

When the following appear on the LEFT of
No. 2—Main Female
————•·•————

The Past

No. 1 —   **Main Male:** Distance between lovers, a risk of separation; the female querent had turned the page.

No. 3 —   **Marriage:** Major problems in the partnership, the querent is single, she had been through a breakup, letting go of a relationship.

No. 4 —   **A Meeting:** A meeting, an event has taken place, taking distance from a group of people, leaving a meet-up.

No. 5 —   **The Good Lord:** Turning away from an elder person, contact with an elder is difficult, father/daughter relationship issue.

No. 6 —   **The Good Lady:** Turning away from an elder person, contact with an elder is difficult, mother/daughter relationship issue.

No. 7 —   **A Pleasant Letter:** A message received, past communication, past conversation.

No. 8 —   **False Person:** Away from Enemy. A rival and cunning dangerous person from the past.

No. 9 —   **A Change:** A recent change, recent move or relocation; a plan occurred.

No. 10 —   **A Journey:** The querent has left a person, place, or situation. A recent travel, a planned trip doesn't turn out the way it was hoped.

No. 11 —   **Lot of Money:** Financial crisis, money goes, the querent does not see this opportunity, the querent turns his back to a positive transaction.

No. 12 —   **A Rich Girl:** Disputes with a daughter, a sister, or any young female relative; turning away to a young female, a generation gap.

No. 13 —   **A Rich Man:** Disputes with a son, a brother, or any young male relative; turning away to a young male, a generation gap.

No. 14 —   **Sad News:** Negative or sad news received, depression is over, letting go of sadness.

No. 15 —   **Success in Love:** The Main Female was in love. A love affair ended, a positive relationship from the past.

No. 16 —   **His Thoughts:** The seeker is no longer preoccupied; she has been through a period of reflection, and a solution has been found.

No. 17 —   **A Gift:** External circumstances has brought joy, the querent was visited, a gift received.

No. 18 — **Small Child:** Abortion, miscarriage. Children are a source of worry; not the right time for a new beginning.

No. 19 — **A Funeral:** The querent lost someone, something is now buried, a break free, coming through a transformation, coming through grief.

No. 20 — **The House:** Selling a property. The Main Female left the safety of her home.

No. 21 — **The Living Room:** Not feeling at home, feeling rejected, leaving the comfort behind.

No. 22 — **A Military:** Official matters are over; leaving the uniform.

No. 23 — **The Court:** Official matters are regulated; the Main Female was wrong.

No. 24 — **The Thievery:** Something or someone was taken away from the Main Female, and the thief escaped.

No. 25 — **High Honours:** The Main Female is educated; she has good reputation and is acknowledged for her talents.

No. 26 — **Big Luck:** Unlucky situation, unfaithful outcome, a failure.

No. 27 — **Unexpected Money:** The Main Female concluded a contract; she has sold her work and received an unexpected sum of money.

No. 28 — **Expectation:** Patience is over; the querent has met a middle-aged woman. In the past she had some sort of expectation.

No. 29 — **The Prison:** The Main Female was lonely, experiencing a lack of freedom and loneliness. With other cards related to health, she could have been admitted to a hospital for treatment.

No. 30 — **Legal Matters:** The Main Female was wrong; the lawyer is not in favor of the querent.

No. 31 — **Short Illness:** Recovery from a short illness, health impairment.

No. 32 — **Grief and Sorrow:** Been through difficult time, out of a depression, healing from addiction.

No. 33 — **Murky Thoughts:** Disenchantment, leaving the drama queen behind.

No. 34 — **Occupation:** Distancing oneself from work, or the Main Female had been working hard lately.

No. 35 — **A Long Road:** Was away to a distant destination. Has shown a lot of patience or was out of patience.

No. 36 — **Hope, Big Water:** Main Female lost hope, coming from abroad in a foreign land, feeling hopeful, a dream had manifested into reality.

When the following appear on the RIGHT of
No. 2—Main Female

The Future

No. 1 — **Main Male:** Harmonious relationship, meeting a significant man, future partner to come, a positive start, a time of sharing and discovery.

No. 3 — **Marriage:** Happily married woman; the querent is looking forward to a commitment. A partnership is on its way; a positive deal or contract.

No. 4 — **A Meeting:** An appointment, a social gathering, an event, meeting a group.

No. 5 — **The Good Lord:** Dealing with an older man, a supportive friend, a father.

No. 6 — **The Good Lady:** Dealing with an older woman, supportive female friend.

No. 7 — **A Pleasant Letter:** Good news to come, positive correspondence, positive phone calls.

No. 8 — **False Person:** Enemy, rival, cunning dangerous person around you, pay attention!

No. 9 — **A Change:** A change is imminent, the Main Female will move or relocation, a planned change will succeed.

No. 10 — **A Journey:** Planned change will succeed, a positive trip, embarking for a journey.

No. 11 — **Lot of Money:** Financial stability, money comes in, wealth and abundance, luxury.

No. 12 — **A Rich Girl:** Interaction with a daughter, a sister, or any young female relative. Closeness with a young female, a young lover.

No. 13 — **A Rich Man:** Interaction with a son, a brother, or any young male relative. Closeness with a young male, a young lover.

No. 14 — **Sad News:** Receiving negative news, a depressed mood, dealing with some bad news.

No. 15 — **Success in Love:** The Main Female falls in love. A love affair, a happy and positive love life.

No. 16 — **His Thoughts:** The seeker is preoccupied, very thoughtful. A lot going on in his mind.

No. 17 — **A Gift:** External circumstances bring joy, a gift, a pleasant visit.

No. 18 — **Small Child:** A new beginning, a pregnancy. The querent is innocent.

No. 19 — **A Funeral:** An ending, a separation, assisting a funeral service.

No. 20 — **The House:** Buying a property; a cozy woman, family house.

No. 21 — **The Living Room:** The querent feels at home, the querent's personal space.

No. 22 — **A Military:** Official matters are on the agenda, encountering someone wearing a uniform.

No. 23 — **The Court:** A final decision, justice triumph, official matter will be regulated.

No. 24 — **The Thievery:** Recovering a lost object, the thief is caught.

No. 25 — **High Honours:** The querent is successful; she receives recognition. A job promotion.

No. 26 — **Big Luck:** The querent is lucky; she can expect happy outcome and lot of success in her ventures.

No. 27 — **Unexpected Money:** A windfall, contracts well negotiated are now paying off, unexpected happy surprise.

No. 28 — **Expectation:** The querent is patient and has strong desires; the next card will say what kind of expectation she has.

No. 29 — **The Prison:** The querent is restricted in her actions. Loneliness, locked away, correctional facility, standstill, stagnation.

No. 30 — **Legal Matters:** Seeing a lawyer, seeking expertise, dealing with legal matters; the Main Female knows the law and her rights perfectly.

No. 31 — **Short Illness:** Weak health condition, fever, small infection, light depression, need to rest, need to sleep.

No. 32 — **Grief and Sorrow:** A difficult time to come, problems and difficulties pile up in front of you. A pattern, a depression, an addiction.

No. 33 — **Murky Thoughts:** Negative mood, lost in fear, drama queen, negative thinking, losing hope.

No. 34 — **Occupation:** Hardworking, motivated, ambitious woman, a job offer.

No. 35 — **A Long Road:** Traveling to a distant destination. Patience—things will not happen overnight.

No. 36 — **Hope, Big Water:** Traveling abroad, crossing waters; the predicted event will happen in a foreign land; feeling hopeful.

When the following appear on the TOP of
No. 2—Main Female

On the Mind

No. 1 —   **Main Male:** She is thinking of a particular man—her husband, her partner, a significant man in her life.

No. 3 —   **Marriage:** Main female dreams of a harmonious relationship, thinking about a future partnership or deal.

No. 4 —   **A Meeting:** Thinking of an appointment, a social gathering, an event, meeting a group.

No. 5 —   **The Good Lord:** Thinking about an older man, a supportive friend, a father.

No. 6 —   **The Good Lady:** Thinking about an older woman, supportive female friend, a mother.

No. 7 —   **A Pleasant Letter:** The querent longs for better communication. Thinking about a message or a correspondence.

No. 8 —   **False Person:** Thinking about an enemy, a rival; a cunning, dangerous person.

No. 9 —   **A Change:** Thinking about a change, the Main Female thinks about a move or a relocation.

No. 10 —   **A Journey:** Thinking about a planned change, about a trip. Longing for a particular destination.

No. 11 —   **Lot of Money:** The querent thinks about financial stability, constantly thinking about his finances; money is very important for the querent.

No. 12 —   **A Rich Girl:** Thinking about a daughter, a sister, or any young female relative; thinking of a young lover.

No. 13 —   **A Rich Man:** Thinking about a son, a brother, or any young male relative; thinking of a young lover.

No. 14 —   **Sad News:** Sorrowful thoughts, fear of bad news, negative thoughts.

No. 15 —   **Success in Love:** Thinking about success, thinking about her love life, her couple.

No. 16 —   **His Thoughts:** The seeker is thinking a lot, her mind is busy, she is making plans.

No. 17 —   **A Gift:** Thinking about a gift, thoughts about a pleasant visit.

No. 18 —   **Small Child:** Thinking of a new beginning, innocent thoughts, naive thoughts, planning something new, thinking of a baby.

No. 19 — **A Funeral:** Thinking of an ending, of a separation; thinking of a funeral.

No. 20 — **The House:** Thinking about a property, of constructing something.

No. 21 — **The Living Room:** Thinking of his private life, thinking about things going on around the house.

No. 22 — **A Military:** A feeling of being controlled, thinking about a strategy, making up a battle plan.

No. 23 — **The Court:** Thinking of a legal issue, thinking about an important decision, thinking of a deadline.

No. 24 — **The Thievery:** Thinking of a lost object, reviewing a loss; the Main Female thinks about taking something away.

No. 25 — **High Honours:** The querent thinks about studying; she is intelligent and aware of her talents and capacities.

No. 26 — **Big Luck:** The querent thinks of his luck, of the various doors opening before her.

No. 27 — **Unexpected Money:** The querent thinks about a contract, about a lucrative deal; she may also be worried by her finances at the moment.

No. 28 — **Expectation:** Thinking of a middle-aged woman, thinking about her goals and motives, thinking about the future of things.

No. 29 — **The Prison:** The querent is thinking about her loneliness; she dreams of freedom.

No. 30 — **Legal Matters:** Considering the help of a lawyer, considering legal dispute.

No. 31 — **Short Illness:** Thinking about his weak health condition, insomnia, the querent should uplift his thoughts in this situation.

No. 32 — **Grief and Sorrow:** Thinking of a difficult time to come, problems and difficulties are piling up; facing a depression, even an addiction.

No. 33 — **Murky Thoughts:** Negative mood, lost in fear, drama queen, negative thinking.

No. 34 — **Occupation:** Preoccupied by her work; the querent's job involves a lot of her logic and intelligence.

No. 35 — **A Long Road:** Thinking of a distant destination; the querent likes to plan things in advance.

No. 36 — **Hope, Big Water:** Fascinated by foreign culture, needs to ground herself.

When the following appear at the BOTTOM of
No. 2—Main Female

Has Achieved

No. 1 —   **Main Male:** The Main Female has a partner, a husband, or someone significant in her life.

No. 3 —   **Marriage:** The Main Female is a happily married woman; she is in a committed relationship/partnership, achieved positive deals and contracts.

No. 4 —   **A Meeting:** Is a very social person, involved in many events, gathering, and parties.

No. 5 —   **The Good Lord:** Is a good person, supportive of her friend.

No. 6 —   **The Good Lady:** Is a good person, supportive of her friend, and a good mother.

No. 7 —   **A Pleasant Letter:** Has a pleasant personality, communicates a lot with others, and is often the bearer of good news.

No. 8 —   **False Person:** The querent may be sabotaging herself; she is her own rival. She has cunning personality and needs to change the way she behaves in life.

No. 9 —   **A Change:** She is a changed woman; she has been through the whole process, even relocating.

No. 10 —   **A Journey:** Our querent is a kind of gypsy, always on the road; her work may involve traveling.

No. 11 —   **Lot of Money:** Has a financial stability, she sits on money, she may be someone who controls every penny spent.

No. 12 —   **A Rich Girl:** Is close to her daughter, sister, or any young female relative. She may be acting like a spoiled child.

No. 13 —   **A Rich Man:** Is close to her son, brother, or any young male relative. She may be acting like a spoiled child.

No. 14 —   **Sad News:** Has a displeasing personality, complains about everything, and is often the bearer of bad news.

No. 15 —   **Success in Love:** The Main Female is a loyal partner, tied to her intention. She is respectful of her relationship, can be trusted at 100%.

No. 16 —   **His Thoughts:** Is more of an action woman than someone who planned things in advance; she is more logical than practical.

No. 17 —   **A Gift:** Loves to give and receive, with a surprising personality, and known to be a gift to others.

No. 18 — **Small Child:** Has achieved a new beginning, is a mother to come; can also be someone with a naive personality.

No. 19 — **A Funeral:** Closely experienced an ending, a separation, or death.

No. 20 — **The House:** The Main Female is the owner of her property, a cozy woman; she is a family girl, tied to family values.

No. 21 — **The Living Room:** Is a secretive woman, protecting her privacy and intimacy, very attached to her home.

No. 22 — **A Military:** Is someone who wears a uniform; she likes discipline and order, ruling her life and business with righteousness.

No. 23 — **The Court:** High minded, the consultant is someone who has principles. She always honors her deadlines.

No. 24 — **The Thievery:** The querent is someone who takes things away; she tends to steal from other people and snatches what she wants.

No. 25 — **High Honours:** The querent is acknowledged and enjoys a good reputation and is seen as a leader.

No. 26 — **Big Luck:** The querent is a lucky woman; she acknowledges it and uses her luck in all of her ventures.

No. 27 — **Unexpected Money:** Our querent is someone who deals well with her contract, and her income is constantly increasing.

No. 28 — **Expectation:** Patience is a virtue for our querent; she is always alert, paying attention to what is on the horizon.

No. 29 — **The Prison:** The querent is a solitary; she may be sabotaging herself.

No. 30 — **Legal Matters:** The querent is avid for expert counsel and advice and uses her wisdom to restore peace and happiness.

No. 31 — **Short Illness:** The Main Female is an insomniac and does not enjoy good health. She may have sexual problems as well.

No. 32 — **Grief and Sorrow:** The querent is a depressive, addicted person.

No. 33 — **Murky Thoughts:** Always sees the glass half empty; likes to keep herself worrying with dark thoughts.

No. 34 — **Occupation:** Hardworking, motivated, ambitious woman.

No. 35 — **A Long Road:** She is patient in her action and awaits for the perfect timing to act.

No. 36 — **Hope, Big Water:** The querent is a gifted one; she may have psychic abilities or some kind of artistic talent.

NO. 3
MARRIAGE

Keywords
Connections, Bonding, Commitment, Unity

*T*he card of 3 Marriage, as you may guess, relates to all kind of commitment and relationships. They can be romantic or business oriented; the surrounding cards will add more details to this bond: what is affecting it or helping it to grow stronger.

When I am conducting a reading that involves a couple, I have a close look at the cards around the 3 Marriage card. It's also a card of fusion; it links and ties two cards together. Like in Lenormand, the positive cards reinforce the goodness and positivity of the reading, while negative ones tend to affect and alter the outcome. Any kind of partnership is positive with the marriage card.

Mantra: I am committed in
all of my relationships.

Influence: Positive

Direction: None

Quick answer: Yes

Topic card: Committed relationship,
marital life

Card No. 3—Marriage with:

No. 1 — **Main Male:** A partnership, a connection with a significant man.

No. 2 — **Main Female:** A partnership, a connection with a significant woman.

No. 4 — **A Meeting:** An encounter during a festivity or celebration.

No. 5 — **The Good Lord:** The groom/bride's father.

No. 6 — **The Good Lady:** The groom/bride's mother.

No. 7 — **A Pleasant Letter:** Good news, positive correspondence, positive phone calls.

No. 8 — **False Person:** One of the partners is not entirely sincere about their feelings and motivation.

No. 9 — **A Change:** The couple wants to move or relocate; they are planning a change.

No. 10 — **A Journey:** One of the partners is leaving; one of them wants to escape this marriage.

No. 11 — **Lot of Money:** This relationship is important and means a lot to the couple.

No. 12 — **A Rich Girl:** Married too young, lack of experience, naivety and ignorance.

No. 13 — **A Rich Man:** Married too young; lack of experience; naivety and ignorance.

No. 14 — **Sad News:** The couple receives negative and sad news; they are depressed.

No. 15 — **Success in Love:** They are truly in love and look forward to this marriage.

No. 16 — **His Thoughts:** The couple is in a place of uncertainty; too many thoughts run through their minds.

No. 17 — **A Gift:** They consider this relationship or partnership as a blessing, a true gift.

No. 18 — **Small Child:** The couple has a childlike attitude; naive, spoiled, exigent, demanding.

No. 19 — **A Funeral:** The couple wants to divorce; they are unhappy; the relationship reaches an end.

No. 20 — **The House:** The couple enjoys family, loves their house and domestic life.

No. 21 — **The Living Room:** The couple needs more intimacy; they need to open up more; the couple's apartment.

No. 22 — **A Military:** A couple in uniform, a dominant relationship, a disciplined and loyal couple.

No. 23 — **The Court:** The couple wants to legalize their relationship; the couple is in a court case, a divorce, a custody.

No. 24 — **The Thievery:** A secretive couple, a fraudulent alliance, two thieves.

No. 25 — **High Honours:** A successful couple, a famous couple, a rewarding alliance, a praised couple.

No. 26 — **Big Luck:** A successful couple, a lucky union, a blessed marriage, a happy ending.

No. 27 — **Unexpected Money:** A good contract, wedding expenses, a contract pays a little, a little money for the couple.

No. 28 — **Expectation:** Expected alliance, expected contract, a patient couple.

No. 29 — **The Prison:** A blocked relationship, stagnant relationship, a blocked contract, isolated couple, lonely couple, lonely relationship.

No. 30 — **Legal Matters:** The couple contacts a lawyer for a divorce; they seek marriage counseling. The couple is dealing with legal matters.

No. 31 — **Short Illness:** They are unhappy in this marriage, an unhealthy relationship, a drama going on.

No. 32 — **Grief and Sorrow:** The couple is sick and needs care.

No. 33 — **Murky Thoughts:** The couple has fearful thoughts, hidden secrets, doubts; has unsolved issues.

No. 34 — **Occupation:** The couple works together, a business deal, a fusion of enterprise.

No. 35 — **A Long Road:** Long-distance relationship, the couple has been waiting patiently for this marriage to happen, long-term commitment.

No. 36 — **Hope, Big Water:** The couple has hope, the couple is spiritually oriented; they have faith in each other.

May these vows and this marriage be blessed.

—RUMI

A REAL READING
WITH THE
MARRIAGE CARD

Rose came to me for a reading; she had been to astrologists a few times but had never experienced a card reading and was quite excited for this new experience. She didn't have any particular question; she was just curious about what was in store for her. I shuffled the deck, invited her to cut the cards, and I started dealing the Grand Tableau. I like to have my client cut the deck. Many readers don't like people touching their cards, but I believe that the querent needs to infuse the cards with their energy, and after each reading I do clear the deck (I explain ways on doing that further along in this book).

The first three cards that came up for Rose were

3 Marriage + 15 Success in Love + 5 The Good Lord

With any doubt, Rose was involved with a man at this moment, and the man was older than her, and she confirmed this. Things looked good as the love card was near, I announced that she will get married to this man, as the 15 Success in Love card falls in the house of the 2 Main Female, and 5 The Good Lord card falls in the house of 3 Marriage (I explained the concept of the house reading on page 231), promising a reinforcement of their bond and relationship.

Three months after the reading, Rose emailed me announcing that her boyfriend had proposed to her, and she was getting married in November.

NO. 4
A MEETING

Keywords

Gathering, Reunion, Get-Together, Encounter

"*Let's* party" is one of the messages of this card. When 4 A Meeting meets your path, it announces a gathering of relatives, friends, or business colleagues. This is a time to enjoy reunions, togetherness, and reconciliations.

I like to use this card when I want to have insights on a group of people; for instance, a study group, people on the internet, my Facebook fans and friends, or my YouTube subscribers. Think about this card as a pack of something. It is also the card of new encounters, new friendship, and of your social life and social connection.

Mantra: I rejoice.

Influence: Neutral

Direction: Man on left, Woman on right

Quick answer: Maybe

Topic card: The group

Card No. 4—A Meeting with

No. 1 — **Main Male:** Meeting and connecting with a significant man.

No. 2 — **Main Female:** Meeting and connecting with a significant woman.

No. 3 — **Marriage:** An encounter during a festivity or celebration.

No. 5 — **The Good Lord:** Meeting and connecting with an older man.

No. 6 — **The Good Lady:** Meeting and connecting with an older woman.

No. 7 — **A Pleasant Letter:** Good news, positive contact and exchange during a meeting, an encounter or a celebration.

No. 8 — **False Person:** Encountering a cunning and dangerous person.

No. 9 — **A Change:** A change in a celebration or in a meeting, a postponed event.

No. 10 — **A Journey:** Going to an event.

No. 11 — **Lot of Money:** An important meeting, gathering, or encounter.

No. 12 — **A Rich Girl:** Meeting and connecting with a young female.

No. 13 — **A Rich Man:** Meeting and connecting with a young male.

No. 14 — **Sad News:** Negative and sad news learned during an event.

No. 15 — **Success in Love:** A date, loving encounter, meeting someone you love.

No. 16 — **His Thoughts:** Meeting of thoughts, a planned party or event.

No. 17 — **A Gift:** A celebration, a birthday, a happy event.

No. 18 — **Small Child:** Baptism, a newborn, a baby shower.

No. 19 — **A Funeral:** A funeral, a nightly meeting.

No. 20 — **The House:** Housewarming, a reunion of family.

No. 21 — **The Living Room:** A private meeting, an intimate celebration.

No. 22 — **A Military:** Appointment with a person in uniform.

No. 23 — **The Court:** A court date, a legal procedure, a witness.

No. 24 — **The Thievery:** Dangerous meeting, being robbed during a celebration.

No. 25 — **High Honours:** A reward, a recognition of some kind, a celebration, an acknowledgment graduation ceremony.

No. 26 — **Big Luck:** A lucky encounter, a happy meeting, being in good company.

No. 27 — **Unexpected Money:** Surprising conversation, unexpected reunion.

No. 28 — **Expectation:** Expecting a meeting, a get-together, a party.

No. 29 — **The Prison:** Trapped by a group, a restricted circle of people.

No. 30 — **Legal Matters:** Contacting a lawyer, seeking an expert's advice.

No. 31 — **Short Illness:** Contagious disease, a group of sick people.

No. 32 — **Grief and Sorrow:** Social crisis, a healing circle.

No. 33 — **Murky Thoughts:** Avoiding social events, a resistor to social life.

No. 34 — **Occupation:** Married to his career, meeting a boyfriend/girlfriend at work.

No. 35 — **A Long Road:** Meeting, gathering, or reunion held in another state or country; long-term commitment.

No. 36 — **Hope, Big Water:** A fateful meeting, a social group, a group reading, a psychic fair.

A REAL READING WITH A MEETING CARD

*T*his event happened around the holiday season. I was invited to a dinner and knew in advance that I would be dealing with difficult people, those kinds of people who are always complaining and arguing and who like to be the "Know it all."

I asked the deck how the party would go and what precautions I needed to take. I decided to do a small three-card reading that would give me clear and precise guidance. The cards I've pulled were

8 The False Person + 16 His Thoughts + 15 Success in Love

So, I will have to deal with someone fake, who wears a mask and would have thoughts about me—not the nicest ones—and would be judgmental. The 15 Success in Love card provides a relief, that things are going to go well as long as I acknowledge the fake person and send her loving and positive thoughts. If you know me, I am a prayer guy, and I am a firm believer in the amazing power of prayer, so I was told to close my eyes, call on my angels, and send loving thoughts and blessings to this party and the people assisting with it, and on the foods and drinks, the music, the building, my journey to it—everything!

What happened was that I arrived on time, without any traffic jam—a pure miracle at this time of the year. I was greeted with smiles and gentle attention and recognized the fake person of the party. At the end she told me that she had some preconceived ideas and finally found out she was wrong.

Through my years of reading cards, I can say that a reading is always empowering rather than fatalistic. The cards will always provide advice that will greatly help; you just need to follow the guidance. Easy does it!

THE GOOD LORD

Keywords
Paternal, Helping, Supportive, Loving, Mature

The Good Lord represents an older male: a father, a grandfather, or a father-in-law. In general, The Good Lord exercises a positive influence on the seeker, always there to help. The Good Lord has a great experience of life; he is a precious ally, a peace bearer that is here to help.

Another quality of this card is maturity; I've always seen my beloved Uncle George, an earth angel who gave me my first Lenormand deck twenty-three years ago, as The Good Lord. In a gay reading, the Main Male with The Good Lord are our main characters.

Mantra: I am protected and loved.

Influence: Positive

Direction: Left

Quick answer: Yes

Topic card: Fatherhood, patriarch

When the following appear on the LEFT of
No. 5—The Good Lord

The Future

No. 1 — **Main Male:** The male querent will interact with an older man, a supportive friend, or a father.

No. 2 — **Main Female:** The female querent will interact with an older man, a supportive friend, or a father.

No. 3 — **Marriage:** The older male is getting married or into a business deal.

No. 4 — **A Meeting:** The older male will be part of a social gathering or in meeting a group.

No. 6 — **The Good Lady:** Elderly couple, parents, grandparents, old lovers.

No. 7 — **A Pleasant Letter:** A document, a letter, correspondence, a contract for the older male.

No. 8 — **False Person:** A rival or enemy from the past; an enemy is backstabbing you.

No. 9 — **A Change:** The older male is in the midst of a change.

No. 10 — **A Journey:** The older male embarks on a journey.

No. 11 — **Lot of Money:** A rich older man, a godfather, a protector.

No. 12 — **A Rich Girl:** An older man with a younger woman, father with daughter, granddaughter with grandfather.

No. 13 — **A Rich Man:** An older man with a younger man, father with son, grandson with grandfather.

No. 14 — **Sad News:** Receiving negative news, a depressed mood, dealing with some bad news.

No. 15 — **Success in Love:** The older male falls in love; love affair, a happy and positive love life.

No. 16 — **His Thoughts:** The old man is preoccupied, very thoughtful, a lot going on in his mind.

No. 17 — **A Gift:** External circumstances bring joy, a gift, a pleasant visit.

No. 18 — **Small Child:** A new beginning, a pregnancy; the older man is innocent.

No. 19 — **A Funeral:** An ending, a separation, assisting with a funeral.

No. 20 — **The House:** Buying a property; a cozy man, a family house, a legacy.

No. 21 — **The Living Room:** The older man feels at home; The Good Lord's personal, private space.

No. 22 — **A Military:** Official matters are on the agenda; the older man encounters someone wearing a uniform.

No. 23 — **The Court:** A final decision, justice triumph; official matter will be regulated for the older man.

No. 24 — **The Thievery:** The older man recovers a lost object; the thief is caught.

No. 25 — **High Honours:** The older man is successful, he receives recognition, a promotion may be on the horizon.

No. 26 — **Big Luck:** The older man is lucky; he can expect a happy outcome and lot of success in his ventures.

No. 27 — **Unexpected Money:** A windfall, contracts well negotiated are now paying off for the older man, unexpected happy surprise.

No. 28 — **Expectation:** The older man is patient and has strong desires; the next card will show what kind of expectation he has.

No. 29 — **The Prison:** The older man is restricted in his actions; he is lonely, locked away, in a correctional facility. A standstill, stagnation.

No. 30 — **Legal Matters:** The older man is seeing a lawyer, seeking expertise, dealing with legal matters.

No. 31 — **Short Illness:** The older man has a health condition, fever, small infection, light depression, need to rest, need to sleep.

No. 32 — **Grief and Sorrow:** A difficult time to come for the older man, problems and difficulties pile up in front of him; a pattern, a depression, addiction.

No. 33 — **Murky Thoughts:** The older man is in a negative mood; he is lost in fear and playing drama queen; negative thinking.

No. 34 — **Occupation:** Hardworking, motivated person. The older man is ambitious; a job offer.

No. 35 — **A Long Road:** The older man travels to a distant destination. Patience—things will not happen overnight.

No. 36 — **Hope, Big Water:** Traveling abroad, crossing waters. The predicted event will happen in a foreign land for the older man; feeling hopeful.

When the following appear on the RIGHT of
No. 5—The Good Lord

The Past

No. 1 — **Main Male:** Dealing with an older man, a supportive friend, a father.

No. 2 — **Main Female:** Dealing with an older woman, a supportive friend, a mother.

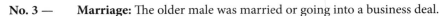

No. 3 —   **Marriage:** The older male was married or going into a business deal.

No. 4 —   **A Meeting:** The older male attended a social gathering.

No. 6 —   **The Good Lady:** Elderly couple, parents, grandparents, old lovers, not on good terms.

No. 7 —   **A Pleasant Letter:** A document, a letter, correspondence, a contract.

No. 8 —   **False Person:** Encountered an old enemy, old rival, a dishonest person.

No. 9 —   **A Change:** The older male was in the midst of a change.

No. 10 —   **A Journey:** The older male has embarked on a journey.

No. 11 —   **Lot of Money:** The Good Lord was a rich man, a businessman, a wealthy person.

No. 12 —   **A Rich Girl:** An older man with a younger woman, father with daughter, granddaughter with grandfather.

No. 13 —   **A Rich Man:** An older man with a younger man, father with son, grandson with grandfather.

No. 14 —   **Sad News:** The older man received negative news; being in a depressed mood, dealing with some bad news.

No. 15 —   **Success in Love:** The older male was in love, in a love affair.

No. 16 —   **His Thoughts:** The old man was preoccupied and very thoughtful; a lot was going on in his mind.

No. 17 —   **A Gift:** External circumstances have brought joy to the elderly man; a gift, a pleasant visit.

No. 18 —   **Small Child:** The older man experienced a new beginning; a pregnancy; the older man was innocent.

No. 19 —   **A Funeral:** An ending, a separation, assisted with a funeral.

No. 20 —   **The House:** Bought a property; a cozy man, a family house, a legacy.

No. 21 —   **The Living Room:** The older man felt at home, but no more; the older man has no private life.

No. 22 —   **A Military:** Official matters were on the agenda; the older man has encountered someone wearing a uniform; was in the military or an officer.

No. 23 —   **The Court:** Justice triumphed; official matters have been regulated for the older man.

No. 24 —   **The Thievery:** The older man has recovered a lost object; the thief was caught.

No. 25 —   **High Honours:** The older man was successful, he has received recognition, a promotion was on the horizon.

No. 26 —   **Big Luck:** The older man was lucky; he was expecting a happy outcome and lot of success in his ventures.

No. 27 — **Unexpected Money:** A windfall, contracts well negotiated have paid off for the older man, unexpected happy surprise.

No. 28 — **Expectation:** The older man was patient and had strong desires; the next card will say what kind of expectation he had.

No. 29 — **The Prison:** The older man was restricted in his actions, alone, locked away; has been in a correctional facility; was in a standstill.

No. 30 — **Legal Matters:** The older man saw a lawyer, has sought expertise, dealt with legal matters.

No. 31 — **Short Illness:** The older man had a health condition, fever, small infections, light depression, need to rest, need to sleep.

No. 32 — **Grief and Sorrow:** The older man went through difficult time, problems; difficulties piled up. A pattern, a depression, addiction.

No. 33 — **Murky Thoughts:** The older man was in a negative mood, felt lost; drama queen, negative thinking.

No. 34 — **Occupation:** Hardworking, motivated; the older man was ambitious; a job was offered.

No. 35 — **A Long Road:** The older man traveled to a distant destination and was shown a lot of patience.

No. 36 — **Hope, Big Water:** Traveled abroad, crossed waters; an event happened in a foreign land for the older man; felt hopeless.

When the following appear on the TOP of
No. 5—The Good Lord

On the Mind

No. 1 — **Main Male:** A father thinks about his son, his grandchild, or the querent.

No. 2 — **Main Female:** A father thinks about his daughter, his grandchild, or the querent.

No. 3 — **Marriage:** The older man dreams of a harmonious relationship; thinking about a future partnership or deal.

No. 4 — **A Meeting:** Thinking of an appointment, a social gathering, an event, meeting a group.

No. 6 — **The Good Lady:** Thinking of an older woman, a supportive female friend.

No. 7 — **A Pleasant Letter:** The older man longs for better communication; thinking of a message or a correspondence.

No. 8 — **False Person:** Is thinking of an enemy, a rival; a cunning, dangerous person.

No. 9 — **A Change:** Thinking of a change, the older man thinks of a move or a relocation.

No. 10 — **A Journey:** Thinking of a change in plans, of a trip. Longing for a particular destination.

No. 11 — **Lot of Money:** The older man thinks of his financial stability, and he is constantly thinking of his finances; money is very important for him.

No. 12 — **A Rich Girl:** Thinking of a daughter, a sister, or any young female relative; thinking of a younger lover.

No. 13 — **A Rich Man:** Thinking of a son, a brother, or any young male relative; thinking of a younger lover.

No. 14 — **Sad News:** Sorrowful thoughts, fear of bad news, negative thoughts.

No. 15 — **Success in Love:** Thinking of success; the older man is thinking of his love life.

No. 16 — **His Thoughts:** The older man is thinking a lot right now.

No. 17 — **A Gift:** Thinking of a gift, thoughts of a pleasant visit.

No. 18 — **Small Child:** Thinking of a new beginning, innocent thoughts, naive thoughts, planning something new, thinking of a baby.

No. 19 — **A Funeral:** Thinking of an ending, of a separation, of a funeral.

No. 20 — **The House:** Thinking of a property, of constructing something. Thinking of the family.

No. 21 — **The Living Room:** Thinking of his private life, thinking of things going on around the house. Thinking of the family.

No. 22 — **A Military:** A feeling of being controlled, thinking about a strategy, making up a battle plan.

No. 23 — **The Court:** Thinking of a legal issue, thinking about an important decision, thinking of a deadline.

No. 24 — **The Thievery:** Thinking of a lost object, reviewing a loss; the older man thinks about taking something away.

No. 25 — **High Honours:** The older man thinks about studying; he is intelligent and aware of his talents and capacities.

No. 26 — **Big Luck:** The older man thinks of his luck, of the various doors opening before him.

No. 27 — **Unexpected Money:** The older man thinks of a contract, of a lucrative deal; he may also be worried by his finances at the moment.

No. 28 — **Expectation:** The older man thinks of a middle-aged woman, thinking about his goals and motives, thinking about the future of things.

No. 29 — **The Prison:** The older man is thinking about his loneliness, dreaming of freedom.

No. 30 — **Legal Matters:** Considering the help of a lawyer, considering legal disputes.

No. 31 — **Short Illness:** Thinking about his weak health condition, insomnia; the querent should uplift his thoughts in this situation.

No. 32 — **Grief and Sorrow:** Thinking of a difficult time to come; problems and difficulties are piling up; facing a depression, even an addiction.

No. 33 — **Murky Thoughts:** Negative mood, lost in fear, drama queen, negative thinking.

No. 34 — **Occupation:** The older man is preoccupied by his work; his job involved a lot of his logic and intelligence.

No. 35 — **A Long Road:** Thinking of a distant destination; the older man plans things in advance.

No. 36 — **Hope, Big Water:** Fascinated by foreign culture; needs to ground himself.

When the following appear at the BOTTOM of
No. 5—The Good Lord

Has Achieved

No. 1 — **Main Male:** The querent is a good man, supportive of his friend, and a good father.

No. 2 — **Main Female:** The querent is a good woman, supportive of his friend, and a good father.

No. 3 — **Marriage:** The older man is a happily married man; he is in a committed relationship/partnership, achieved positive deals and contracts.

No. 4 — **A Meeting:** Is a very social person, involved in events, gathering, and get-togethers.

No. 6 — **The Good Lady:** Is a good person, supportive of her friends.

No. 7 — **A Pleasant Letter:** Has a pleasant personality, communicates a lot with others, and is often the bearer of good news.

No. 8 — **False Person:** The older man may be sabotaging himself. He is his own rival and has a cunning personality and needs to change the way he behaves in life.

No. 9 — **A Change:** He is a changed man; he had been through the whole process, even relocating.

No. 10 —   **A Journey:** The elder man is a kind of gypsy, always on the road; his work may involve travel (e.g., a truck driver).

No. 11 —   **Lot of Money:** A rich older man, a sugar daddy.

No. 12 —   **A Rich Girl:** Is close to his daughter, grandchild, or any young female relative. He may be acting like a spoiled child.

No. 13 —   **A Rich Man:** Is close to his son, grandchild, or any young male relative. He may be acting like a spoiled child.

No. 14 —   **Sad News:** The older man has a displeasing personality, complains about everything, and is often the bearer of bad news.

No. 15 —   **Success in Love:** The older man is a loyal partner, tied to his intention, respectful of his relationship; can be trusted 100%.

No. 16 —   **His Thoughts:** Is more of an action man than someone who plans things in advance; the older man is more logical than practical.

No. 17 —   **A Gift:** Loves to give and receive, has a surprising personality, and is known to be a gift to others.

No. 18 —   **Small Child:** Had achieved new beginning, is a father/grandfather to come, can also be someone with a naive personality.

No. 19 —   **A Funeral:** Closely experienced an ending, a separation, or death.

No. 20 —   **The House:** The older man is the owner of his property; a cozy man, he is a family man, tied to family values.

No. 21 —   **The Living Room:** Is a secretive man, protecting his privacy and intimacy, very attached to his home.

No. 22 —   **A Military:** The older man is someone who wears a uniform; he likes discipline and order, ruling his life and business with righteousness.

No. 23 —   **The Court:** High minded, the older man is someone who has principles; he always honors deadlines.

No. 24 —   **The Thievery:** The older man is someone who takes things away; he tends to steal from other people and snatches what he wants.

No. 25 —   **High Honours:** The older man is acknowledged and enjoys a good reputation, is seen as a leader.

No. 26 —   **Big Luck:** The older man is a lucky man; he acknowledges it and uses his luck in every venture.

No. 27 —   **Unexpected Money:** The older man is someone who deals well with his contract, and his income is constantly increasing.

No. 28 —   **Expectation:** Patience is a virtue for him; he is always alert, paying attention to what is on the horizon.

No. 29 —   **The Prison:** A solitary older man; he may be sabotaging himself.

No. 30 —   **Legal Matters:** The older man is avid with counsel and advice, uses his wisdom to restore peace and happiness.

No. 31 —   **Short Illness:** The older man is an insomniac and does not enjoy good health. He may have sexual problems as well.

No. 32 —   **Grief and Sorrow:** Depressive older man, addicted person.

No. 33 —   **Murky Thoughts:** Always sees the glass half empty, likes to keep himself worrying with dark thoughts.

No. 34 —   **Occupation:** Hardworking, motivated, ambitious man.

No. 35 —   **A Long Road:** He is patient in his action and waits for the perfect timing.

No. 36 —   **Hope, Big Water:** The older man is gifted; he may have psychic abilities or any kind of artistic talent.

NO. 6
THE GOOD LADY

Keywords
Maternal, Helping, Supportive, Loving, Mature

The Good Lady represents an older female: a mother, a grandmother, or a mother-in-law. In general, The Good Lady exercises a positive influence on the seeker and is always there to help through support and counsel. The Good Lady has a great experience of life; she is a precious ally, a peace bearer that is here to help.

Another quality of this card is maturity; The Good Lady can stand for a situation that needs more time to age before it turns into something amazing (like wine, cheese, pickles, etc.).

In a lesbian reading, the 2 Main Female with 6 The Good Lady are our characters.

Mantra: I am protected and love.

Influence: Positive

Direction: Right

Quick answer: Yes

Topic card: Motherhood, matriarch

When the following appear on the LEFT of
No. 6—The Good Lady

The Past

No. 1 — **Main Male:** The male querent dealt with an older woman, a supportive friend, a mother.

No. 2 — **Main Female:** The female querent dealt with an older woman, a supportive friend, a mother.

No. 3 — **Marriage:** The older female was married or was in a business deal.

No. 4 — **A Meeting:** The older female was part of a social gathering or is meeting a group.

No. 5 — **The Good Lord:** Elderly couple, parents, grandparents, old lovers, not on good terms.

No. 7 — **A Pleasant Letter:** A document, a letter, correspondence, or a contract was received

No. 8 — **False Person:** Encountered an old enemy, old rival, a dishonest person.

No. 9 — **A Change:** The older female was in the midst of a change.

No. 10 — **A Journey:** The older female has embarked on a journey.

No. 11 — **Lot of Money:** The Good Lady was a rich woman, a businesswoman, a wealthy person.

No. 12 — **A Rich Girl:** An older woman with a younger woman, mother with daughter, granddaughter with grandmother.

No. 13 — **A Rich Man:** An older woman with a younger man, mother with son, grandson with grandmother.

No. 14 — **Sad News:** The older woman received negative news, is in a depressed mood, dealing with some bad news.

No. 15 — **Success in Love:** The older female was in love, was in a love affair.

No. 16 — **His Thoughts:** The old woman was preoccupied and very thoughtful; a lot was going on in her mind.

No. 17 — **A Gift:** External circumstances have brought joy, a gift, a pleasant visit.

No. 18 — **Small Child:** The older woman experienced a new beginning, a pregnancy; the older woman was innocent.

No. 19 — **A Funeral:** An ending, a separation, assisted a funeral.

No. 20 — **The House:** Bought a property; a cozy woman, a family house, a legacy.

No. 21 — **The Living Room:** The older woman felt at home, but no more.

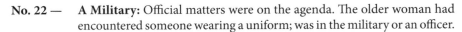

No. 22 —   **A Military:** Official matters were on the agenda. The older woman had encountered someone wearing a uniform; was in the military or an officer.

No. 23 —   **The Court:** Justice triumphed; official matters have been regulated for the older woman.

No. 24 —   **The Thievery:** The older woman has recovered a lost object; the thief was caught.

No. 25 —   **High Honours:** The older woman was successful, she has received recognition, a promotion was on the horizon.

No. 26 —   **Big Luck:** The older woman was lucky; she was expecting a happy outcome and lots of success in her ventures.

No. 27 —   **Unexpected Money:** A windfall, contract well negotiated has paid off for the older woman; unexpected happy surprise.

No. 28 —   **Expectation:** The older woman was patient and has strong desires; the next card will say what kind of expectation she had.

No. 29 —   **The Prison:** The older woman was restricted in her actions, alone, locked away; has been in a correctional facility; was at a standstill.

No. 30 —   **Legal Matters:** The older woman saw a lawyer, has sought expertise, dealt with legal matters.

No. 31 —   **Short Illness:** The older woman had a health condition, fever, small infection, light depression, need to rest.

No. 32 —   **Grief and Sorrow:** The older woman faced a difficulty; problems and difficulties piled up in front of her. A pattern, a depression, addiction.

No. 33 —   **Murky Thoughts:** The older woman was in a negative mood, lost in fear; drama queen, negative thinking.

No. 34 —   **Occupation:** Hardworking, motivated, the older woman was ambitious. A job was offered.

No. 35 —   **A Long Road:** The older woman traveled to a distant destination and was shown a lot of patience.

No. 36 —   **Hope, Big Water:** The older woman traveled abroad, crossed waters. An event happened in a foreign land for the older woman; she felt hopeful.

When the following appear on the RIGHT of
No. 6—The Good Lady

The Future

No. 1 — **Main Male:** The male querent will interact with an older woman, a supportive friend, a mother.

No. 2 — **Main Female:** The female querent will interact with an older woman, a supportive friend, a mother.

No. 3 — **Marriage:** The older female is getting married or into a business deal.

No. 4 — **A Meeting:** The older female will be part of a social gathering or is meeting a group.

No. 5 — **The Good Lord:** Elderly couple, parents, grandparents, old lovers.

No. 7 — **A Pleasant Letter:** A document, letter, correspondence, contract for the older female.

No. 8 — **False Person:** Encountering an old enemy, old rivalry, a dishonest person.

No. 9 — **A Change:** The older female is in the midst of a change.

No. 10 — **A Journey:** The older female embarks on a journey.

No. 11 — **Lot of Money:** A rich older woman, a godmother, a protector.

No. 12 — **A Rich Girl:** An older woman with a younger woman, mother with daughter, granddaughter with grandmother.

No. 13 — **A Rich Man:** An older woman with a younger man, mother with son, grandson with grandmother.

No. 14 — **Sad News:** Receiving negative news, a depressed mood, dealing with some bad news.

No. 15 — **Success in Love:** The older female falls in love. A love affair, a happy and positive love life.

No. 16 — **His Thoughts:** The old woman is preoccupied, very thoughtful; a lot going on in her mind.

No. 17 — **A Gift:** External circumstances bring joy, a gift, a pleasant visit.

No. 18 — **Small Child:** A new beginning, a pregnancy, the older woman is innocent.

No. 19 — **A Funeral:** An ending, a separation, assisting with a funeral service.

No. 20 — **The House:** Buying a property; a cozy woman, a family house, a legacy.

No. 21 — **The Living Room:** The older woman feels at home; the Good Lady's personal space.

No. 22 — **A Military:** Official matters are on the agenda; the older woman encounters someone wearing a uniform.

No. 23 — **The Court:** A final decision, justice triumphs, official matter will be regulated for the older woman.

No. 24 — **The Thievery:** The older woman recovers a lost object; the thief is caught.

No. 25 — **High Honours:** The older woman is successful, she receives recognition, a promotion may be on the horizon.

No. 26 — **Big Luck:** The older woman is lucky; she can expect a happy outcome and lots of success in her ventures.

No. 27 — **Unexpected Money:** A windfall, contracts well negotiated are now paying off for the older woman; unexpected happy surprise.

No. 28 — **Expectation:** The older woman is patient and has strong desires; the next card will say what kind of expectation she has.

No. 29 — **The Prison:** The older woman is restricted in her actions. Loneliness, locked away, correctional facility, standstill, stagnation.

No. 30 — **Legal Matters:** The older woman is seeing a lawyer, seeking expertise, dealing with legal matters.

No. 31 — **Short Illness:** The older woman has a health condition, fever, small infection, light depression, needs to rest, needs to sleep.

No. 32 — **Grief and Sorrow:** A difficult time to come for the older woman; problems and difficulties pile up in front of her; a pattern, a depression, addiction.

No. 33 — **Murky Thoughts:** The older woman is in a negative mood, lost in fear; drama queen, negative thinking.

No. 34 — **Occupation:** Hardworking, motivated, ambitious older woman; a job offer.

No. 35 — **A Long Road:** The older woman travels to a distant destination; patience—things will not happen now.

No. 36 — **Hope, Big Water:** Traveling abroad, crossing waters; event will happen in a foreign land for the older woman; feeling hopeful.

When the following appear on the TOP of
No. 6—The Good Lady

On the Mind

No. 1 — **Main Male:** A mother thinks about his son, his grandchild, or the male querent.

No. 2 — **Main Female:** A mother thinks about her daughter, her grandchild, or the female querent.

No. 3 — **Marriage:** The older woman dreams of a harmonious relationship; thinking about a future partnership or deal.

No. 4 — **A Meeting:** Thinking of an appointment, a social gathering, an event, meeting a group.

No. 5 — **The Good Lord:** Thinking of an older man, supportive male friend.

No. 7 — **A Pleasant Letter:** The older woman longs for better communication. Thinking of a message or a correspondence.

No. 8 — **False Person:** The older woman is thinking of an enemy, a rival, a cunning and dangerous person.

No. 9 — **A Change:** Thinking of a change, the older woman thinks of a move or a relocation.

No. 10 — **A Journey:** Thinking of changing plans, of a trip. Longing for a particular destination.

No. 11 — **Lot of Money:** The older woman thinks of her financial stability, constantly thinking of her finances. Money is very important for her.

No. 12 — **A Rich Girl:** Thinking of a daughter, a sister, or any young female relative; thinking of a young lover.

No. 13 — **A Rich Man:** Thinking of a son, a brother, or any young male relative; thinking of a young lover.

No. 14 — **Sad News:** Sorrowful thoughts, fear of bad news, negative thoughts.

No. 15 — **Success in Love:** Thinking of success, thinking of his love life.

No. 16 — **His Thoughts:** The older woman is thinking a lot right now.

No. 17 — **A Gift:** Thinking of a gift; thoughts of a pleasant visit, pleasant thoughts.

No. 18 — **Small Child:** Thinking of a new beginning, innocent thoughts, naive thoughts, planning something new; thinking of a baby.

No. 19 — **A Funeral:** Thinking of an ending, of a separation; thinking of a funeral.

No. 20 — **The House:** Thinking of a property, of constructing something.

No. 21 — **The Living Room:** Thinking of her private life. Thinking of things going on around the house.

No. 22 — **A Military:** A feeling of being controlled. Thinking about a strategy, making up a battle plan.

No. 23 — **The Court:** Thinking of a legal issue, thinking about an important decision, thinking of a deadline.

No. 24 — **The Thievery:** Thinking of a lost object, reviewing a loss. The older woman thinks about taking something away.

No. 25 — **High Honours:** The older woman thinks of studying; she is intelligent and aware of her talents and capacities.

No. 26 — **Big Luck:** The older woman thinks of his luck, of the various doors opening

No. 27 — **Unexpected Money:** The older woman thinks of a contract, about a lucrative deal; she may also be worried by her finances at the moment.

No. 28 — **Expectation:** The older woman thinks of a middle-aged woman; thinking about her goals and motives. Thinking about the future of things.

No. 29 — **The Prison:** The older woman is thinking about her loneliness, dreaming of freedom.

No. 30 — **Legal Matters:** Considering the help of a lawyer, considering legal dispute.

No. 31 — **Short Illness:** Thinking about her weak health condition. Insomnia. The querent should uplift his/her thought in this situation.

No. 32 — **Grief and Sorrow:** Thinking of a difficult time to come; problems and difficulties are piling up; facing a depression, even an addiction.

No. 33 — **Murky Thoughts:** Negative mood, lost in fear, drama queen, negative thinking.

No. 34 — **Occupation:** Preoccupied by her work, the older woman's job involves a lot of his logic and intelligence.

No. 35 — **A Long Road:** Thinking of a distant destination, the older woman plans things in advance.

No. 36 — **Hope, Big Water:** The older lady is fascinated by foreign culture, needs to ground herself.

When the following appear at the BOTTOM of
No. 6—The Good Lady

Has Achieved

No. 1 — **Main Male:** The querent is a good man, supportive of his friend, and a good father.

No. 2 — **Main Female:** The querent is a good woman, supportive of his friend, and a good mother.

No. 3 — **Marriage:** The older woman is happily married; she is in a committed relationship/partnership, achieved positive deal and contracts.

No. 4 — **A Meeting:** Is a very social person, involved in an event, gathering, and get-together.

No. 5 — **The Good Lord:** Is a good person, supportive of her friend.

No. 7 — **A Pleasant Letter:** Has a pleasant personality; communicates a lot with others and is often the bearer of good news.

No. 8 — **False Person:** The older woman may be sabotaging herself; she is her own rival. She has a cunning personality and needs to change the way she behaves in life.

No. 9 — **A Change:** She is a changed woman; she had been through the whole process, even relocating.

No. 10 — **A Journey:** The older woman is a kind of gypsy, always on the road; her work may involve travel.

No. 11 — **Lot of Money:** A rich older woman, a cougar.

No. 12 — **A Rich Girl:** The older lady is close to her daughter, her grandchild, or any young female relative. She may be acting like a spoiled child.

No. 13 — **A Rich Man:** The older lady is close to her son, her grandchild, or any young male relative. She may be acting like a spoiled child.

No. 14 — **Sad News:** The older woman has a displeasing personality, complains about everything, and is often the bearer of bad news.

No. 15 — **Success in Love:** The older woman is a loyal partner, tied to her intention, respectful of his relationship; can be trusted at 100%.

No. 16 — **His Thoughts:** The older lady is more of an action girl than someone who planned things in advance; she is more logical than practical.

No. 17 — **A Gift:** Loves to give and receive, with a surprising personality; known to be a gift to others.

No. 18 — **Small Child:** The older lady has achieved a new beginning, is a mother/grandmother to come, can also be someone with a naive personality.

No. 19 — **A Funeral:** The older lady closely experienced an ending, a separation, or death.

No. 20 — **The House:** The older lady is the owner of her property, a cozy woman; she is a family woman, tied to family values.

No. 21 — **The Living Room:** The older lady is a secretive woman, protecting her privacy and intimacy, very attached to her home.

No. 22 — **A Military:** The older lady is someone who wears a uniform; she likes discipline and order, ruling her life and business with righteousness.

No. 23 — **The Court:** High minded, the older lady is someone who has principles; she always honors deadlines.

No. 24 — **The Thievery:** The older woman is someone who takes things away; she tends to steal from other people and snatches what she wants.

No. 25 — **High Honours:** The older woman is acknowledged, enjoys a good reputation, and is seen as a leader.

No. 26 —   **Big Luck:** The older woman is a lucky girl; she acknowledges it and uses her luck in every one of her ventures.

No. 27 —   **Unexpected Money:** The older woman is someone who deals well with her contracts, and her income is constantly increasing.

No. 28 —   **Expectation:** Patience is a virtue for her; she is always alert, paying attention to what is on the horizon.

No. 29 —   **The Prison:** A solitary older woman, she may be sabotaging herself.

No. 30 —   **Legal Matters:** The older woman is avid of counsel and advice and uses her wisdom to restore peace and happiness.

No. 31 —   **Short Illness:** The older lady is an insomniac and does not enjoy good health. She may have sexual problems as well.

No. 32 —   **Grief and Sorrow:** Depressive older woman, addicted person.

No. 33 —   **Murky Thoughts:** Always sees the glass half empty. Likes to keep herself worrying with dark thoughts.

No. 34 —   **Occupation:** Hardworking, motivated, ambitious woman.

No. 35 —   **A Long Road:** The older lady is patient in her action and waits for the perfect timing.

No. 36 —   **Hope, Big Water:** The older woman is a gifted one; she may have psychic abilities or any kind of artistic talent.

We are born of love;
love is our mother.

—RUMI

A PLEASANT LETTER

Keywords
News, Announcement, Documents, Messages, Memos, Letters

A Pleasant Letter is about all forms of communication: written messages and correspondences, spoken communication, phone calls, etc. In a lesser degree, the card that relates to a document, a memo, plans, and all kinds of reports. Like all neutral cards, the surrounding cards will color its meaning from positive to extra positive or from positive to negative.

Mantra: I receive wonderful news.

Influence: Positive

Direction: None

Quick answer: Yes

Topic card: Correspondence and paperwork

Card No. 7—A Pleasant Letter with

No. 1 — **Main Male:** Past communication, unpleasant message or phone calls for the male querent.

No. 2 — **Main Female:** Good news, news to come, positive correspondence, positive phone calls for the female querent.

No. 3 — **Marriage:** Good news and messages about a deal, a wedding invitation, a business contract.

No. 4 — **A Meeting:** Good news, positive contact and exchange during a meeting, an encounter or a celebration.

No. 5 — **The Good Lord:** Positive document, letter, correspondence, contract from a positive older man.

No. 6 — **The Good Lady:** Positive document, letter, correspondence, contract from a positive older woman.

No. 8 — **False Person:** A misleading message, an enemy receives a message, pay attention the documents.

No. 9 — **A Change:** A positive change, the good news changes everything, a positive outcome.

No. 10 — **A Journey:** Travel document, driver's license, car registration, insurance policy.

No. 11 — **Lot of Money:** Loan/credit agreement, positive money transaction, receiving money.

No. 12 — **A Rich Girl:** Message from a younger woman, correspondence or document related to her, contacting a young woman, message from a longtime lover.

No. 13 — **A Rich Man:** Message from a younger man, correspondence or document related to him, contacting a young man, message from a longtime lover.

No. 14 — **Sad News:** Bad news; deprive the pleasant letter of its positive omen.

No. 15 — **Success in Love:** A love letter, a declaration of love and appreciation.

No. 16 — **His Thoughts:** Things that are only in the mind; plans, diagram, drawing, design. Things that are not yet on paper.

No. 17 — **A Gift:** A godsend message, a parcel containing a present, a positive surprise, a pleasant visit.

No. 18 — **Small Child:** Birth announcement, a birth certificate, a message comes early in the morning.

No. 19 — **A Funeral:** Death certificate, death announcement; a message comes late at night.

No. 20 — **The House:** Title deeds, good news from family, real-estate contract.

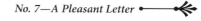

No. 21 — **The Living Room:** Private message, personal correspondence, personal diary.

No. 22 — **A Military:** Official letter, conversation or letter from a person in uniform, a police report.

No. 23 — **The Court:** Legal document, a notification from the court, a court date, a witness statement.

No. 24 — **The Thievery:** A lost document, a false statement, a negative letter.

No. 25 — **High Honours:** A certificate, an award, a diploma, a business deal.

No. 26 — **Big Luck:** A message promises great fortune, a positive turn of events, exceptional news, an important document.

No. 27 — **Unexpected Money:** Unexpected correspondence, a refund, coupon, discount code.

No. 28 — **Expectation:** Messages from a middle-aged woman, expecting a call, a letter, a message.

No. 29 — **The Prison:** A legal prohibition, a blocked message, protection order notice.

No. 30 — **Legal Matters:** Legal document, letter from an attorney, notice of litigation.

No. 31 — **Short Illness:** Checkup results, health results, a health catalog or brochure. A disrupting communication.

No. 32 — **Grief and Sorrow:** Sad news, fear of a particular message or document, writing about grief, a message of emotional distress.

No. 33 — **Murky Thoughts:** A message of emotional distress, a message brought out a lot of doubt and negative thoughts.

No. 34 — **Occupation:** Work-related document, a writer, a poet, a blogger, someone who expresses himself through creative writing.

No. 35 — **A Long Road:** An awaited message or document, a document that comes from far away.

No. 36 — **Hope, Big Water:** A message of hope, boat or cruise tickets, a letter from a foreign country.

A REAL READING WITH
A PLEASANT LETTER

*W*ith my work, I receive all sorts of letters and papers, from contracts to articles, clients' testimonials and letters, and online orders. It happens from time to time that one of my parcels or correspondences does not arrive to me on time or gets lost during distribution. In this case, I use my cards to locate the parcel, and 7 A Pleasant Letter is my focus card for the subject. I read the two cards that sandwich 7 A Pleasant Letter card.

There's an example for a deck of mine that was taking a while to arrive to me; the cards I pulled were

29 The Prison + 7 A Pleasant Letter + 10 A Journey

My interpretation is that my parcel is blocked (29 The Prison)—at customs maybe—and I should drive there (10 A Journey) to find out more information. I did exactly that and found that the parcel was blocked because the invoice was missing, and customs could not evaluate the parcel.

*Raise your words,
not your voice.
It is rain that grows flowers,
not thunder.*

—RUMI

FALSE PERSON

Keywords
Falsehood, Lies, Enemy, Danger, Wrong, Imposter

False Person is a card of adversity; a person/situation may be against you. Pay attention, as not everything that glitters is gold! As a person, it can indicate someone deceitful or jealous, or someone who brings confusion and troubles along; it may be the right time to question his/her motives and find the reason why this person is being so insincere.

As a situation, things are definitely not in your favor; you may make the wrong decision or be involved with a wrong action.

Remember that this person or situation will always try to confuse and harm you; be observant and vigilant!

Mantra: No person or place has any power over me.

Influence: Negative

Direction: Left

Quick answer: No

Topic card: Enemy and danger

When the following appear on the LEFT of
No. 8—False Person

The Future

No. 1 —   **Main Male:** An enemy is stabbing the Main Male in the back; pay attention to the people around you. White teeth—black heart, a wronged man.

No. 2 —   **Main Female:** Dealing with a dangerous woman, confronting an enemy, being in an argument, a challenging situation, a wrong woman.

No. 3 —   **Marriage:** An envious woman, jealous of your soul-mated relationship, she may be manipulating one of the partners; a wrong commitment.

No. 4 —   **A Meeting:** A wrong appointment, a social gathering or event that may hide an enemy, argument in a reunion.

No. 5 —   **The Good Lord:** A wrong older man, manipulating a man; the False Person will soon encounter an elderly man.

No. 6 —   **The Good Lady:** The imposter is dealing with a generous good female; a vicious interaction, vice vs. virtue.

No. 7 —   **A Pleasant Letter:** A wrong letter, bad news, news or correspondence from a fraud, negative phone calls.

No. 9 —   **A Change:** Wrong direction, a wrong relocation, moving toward an enemy, jump into the lion's den.

No. 10 —   **A Journey:** Wrong path, a negative trip, embarking for a dangerous journey, hidden default with a car.

No. 11 —   **Lot of Money:** Fraud going around; be careful with your transactions; a transaction is avoided.

No. 12 —   **A Rich Girl:** Stepdaughter, adopted girl, a false friend, a fake, a liar, a wolf disguised in sheep's clothing.

No. 13 —   **A Rich Man:** Stepson, adopted son, a false friend, a fake, a liar, a wolf disguised in sheep's clothing.

No. 14 —   **Sad News:** A disappointment, a wrong or false result, bad news.

No. 15 —   **Success in Love:** Dishonest partner, an affair, a wrong relationship.

No. 16 —   **His Thoughts:** Wrong thoughts, illusion, confused thoughts.

No. 17 —   **A Gift:** A wrong gift, a wrong visit, unpleasant surprise, an enemy in disguise.

No. 18 —   **Small Child:** Adopted child, wrong decision, falsehood, childhood jealousy.

No. 19 — **A Funeral:** Termination, separation, an ending through suffering.

No. 20 — **The House:** Negative environment, bad neighborhood, an illusion of security, traitor in the family.

No. 21 — **The Living Room:** Envious; traitors are close to you; pay attention to your surroundings; a wrong environment.

No. 22 — **A Military:** An imposter, he is not what he pretends to be; someone disguised and playing a role.

No. 23 — **The Court:** Wrong decision, false witness, verdict based on wrong information, a corrupted lawyer.

No. 24 — **The Thievery:** Dangerous person, a fraud, a theft, an abuser, a fugitive, a recidivist.

No. 25 — **High Honours:** Fake diploma, an enemy preventing a good thing to come along, an enemy to your success.

No. 26 — **Big Luck:** Someone is blocking your fortune, your happiness is in the hand of a traitor, someone is sabotaging your progression.

No. 27 — **Unexpected Money:** Dealing with cunning people, a wrong contract, a blocked sum of money.

No. 28 — **Expectation:** An enemy has some expectation; someone is watching from afar; negative expectation, wrong expectation.

No. 29 — **The Prison:** An enemy is blocked, the traitor is punished, the False Person is alone.

No. 30 — **Legal Matters:** False lawyer, wrong expertise, incorrect advice.

No. 31 — **Short Illness:** A wrong diagnosis, pretending to be sick, mental illness, being bullied.

No. 32 — **Grief and Sorrow:** An enemy is causing much pain through gossip and harassment; fake despair, drama queen.

No. 33 — **Murky Thoughts:** Negative mood; someone is bringing your morale down; negative thinking.

No. 34 — **Occupation:** Traitor in the workplace, manipulation in the work environment, unfaithful colleague.

No. 35 — **A Long Road:** Leaving is the wrong decision, an enemy awaits patiently, traveling far away is not a good thing.

No. 36 — **Hope, Big Water:** Traveling abroad or immigrating is wrong, a misconception, false hope.

When the following appear on the RIGHT of
No. 8—False Person

The Past

No. 1 —   **Main Male:** An enemy is stabbing the Main Male in the back; pay attention to the people around you; white teeth—black heart, a wronged man from the past.

No. 2 —   **Main Female:** Dealing with a dangerous woman, confronting an enemy, being in an argument, a challenging situation, a wrong woman from the past.

No. 3 —   **Marriage:** An envious woman, jealous of your soul-mated relationship; she had been manipulating one of the partners in the past.

No. 4 —   **A Meeting:** A wrong appointment, a social gathering or event that was hiding an enemy, argument happened in a reunion.

No. 5 —   **The Good Lord:** A wrong older man, manipulating a man; the False Person had encounter an elderly man.

No. 6 —   **The Good Lady:** The imposter dealt with a generous good female; an interaction, vice vs. virtue.

No. 7 —   **A Pleasant Letter:** A wrong letter, bad news, news or correspondence from a fraud, negative phone calls.

No. 9 —   **A Change:** Wrong decision was made in the past direction, a wrong relocation; has moved toward an enemy, jumped into the lion's den.

No. 10 —   **A Journey:** Wrong decision was made in the past direction, a past negative trip; embarked on a dangerous journey, hidden default with a car.

No. 11 —   **Lot of Money:** A fraud had been going around; be careful with your transactions; a transaction was avoided.

No. 12 —   **A Rich Girl:** Stepdaughter, adopted girl, a false friend, a fake, a liar, wolf disguised in sheep's clothing.

No. 13 —   **A Rich Man:** Stepson, adopted son, a false friend, a fake, a liar, wolf disguised in sheep's clothing.

No. 14 —   **Sad News:** A disappointment, a wrong or false result, bad news.

No. 15 —   **Success in Love:** Dishonest partner, an affair, a wrong relationship.

No. 16 —   **His Thoughts:** Wrong thought, illusion, confused thoughts.

No. 17 —   **A Gift:** A wrong gift, a wrong visit, a bad surprise, an enemy in disguise from the past.

No. 18 —   **Small Child:** Adopted child, wrong decision, falsehood, childhood jealousy.

No. 19 — **A Funeral:** Termination, separation, an ending through suffering.

No. 20 — **The House:** Negative environment, bad neighborhood, an illusion of security, traitor in the family.

No. 21 — **The Living Room:** Envious; traitors are close to you; pay attention to your surroundings; a wrong environment.

No. 22 — **A Military:** An imposter, he is not what he pretends to be; someone disguised and playing a role.

No. 23 — **The Court:** Wrong decision, false witness, verdict based on wrong information, a corrupt lawyer.

No. 24 — **The Thievery:** Dangerous person, a fraud, a theft, an abuser, a fugitive, a recidivist.

No. 25 — **High Honours:** Fake diplomat, an enemy preventing good things to come along, an enemy to your success.

No. 26 — **Big Luck:** Someone is blocking your fortune, your happiness is in the hand of a traitor, someone is sabotaging your progression.

No. 27 — **Unexpected Money:** Dealing with cunning people, a wrong contract, a sum of money blocked.

No. 28 — **Expectation:** An enemy has some expectation, someone is watching from afar; negative expectation, wrong expectation.

No. 29 — **The Prison:** An enemy is blocked, the traitor is punished, the False Person is alone.

No. 30 — **Legal Matters:** False lawyer, wrong expertise, incorrect advice.

No. 31 — **Short Illness:** A wrong diagnosis, pretending to be sick, mental illness, being bullied.

No. 32 — **Grief and Sorrow:** An enemy caused much pain through gossip and harassment; fake despair, drama queen.

No. 33 — **Murky Thoughts:** Negative mood, someone is bringing your morale down, negative thinking.

No. 34 — **Occupation:** Traitor in the workplace, manipulation in the work environment, unfaithful colleague.

No. 35 — **A Long Road:** Leaving was a wrong decision, an enemy waited patiently, traveling far away is not a good thing.

No. 36 — **Hope, Big Water:** Traveling abroad or immigrating was wrong, a misconception, false hope.

When the following appear on the TOP of
No. 8—False Person

On the Mind

No. 1 —   **Main Male:** The False Person is thinking of the querent; how she can wrong him.

No. 2 —   **Main Female:** The False Person is thinking of the querent; how she can wrong her.

No. 3 —   **Marriage:** The False Person thinks about a couple; how she can manipulate these persons.

No. 4 —   **A Meeting:** The False Person is thinking of an appointment; how she can turn this social gathering in her advantage and make the group believe what she wants.

No. 5 —   **The Good Lord:** The False person is thinking of an older man, a father; how she can use this person to her advantage.

No. 6 —   **The Good Lady:** The False Person is thinking of an older woman, a mother; how she can use this person to her advantage.

No. 7 —   **A Pleasant Letter:** The False Person thinks of a particular message or letter; she may want to use that to her advantage.

No. 9 —   **A Change:** The False person is thinking of a change, of a move, or a relocation.

No. 10 —   **A Journey:** The dishonest person is planning a change, a trip, going away, or a retreat to prepare her plans.

No. 11 —   **Lot of Money:** The False Person thinks of money, and how she can obtain more or use that money in her plans. Money is very important to the False Person.

No. 12 —   **A Rich Girl:** The dishonest person is thinking of a daughter, a sister, or any young female relative.

No. 13 —   **A Rich Man:** The False Person is thinking of a son, a brother, or any young male relative; thinking of a young lover.

No. 14 —   **Sad News:** The False Person has sorrowful thoughts; she fears bad news, holds on to negative thoughts.

No. 15 —   **Success in Love:** The False Person may manipulate love to her advantage, using seduction to obtain favors.

No. 16 —   **His Thoughts:** The dishonest person is thinking a lot right now.

No. 17 —   **A Gift:** The False Person thinks about a visit; a gift of how she can obtain what she wants through manipulation.

No. 18 — **Small Child:** The False Person has naive thoughts and acts like a spoiled child.

No. 19 — **A Funeral:** The dishonest person is thinking of an ending, of a separation, of a funeral.

No. 20 — **The House:** The False Person is thinking of a property, of constructing something.

No. 21 — **The Living Room:** The False Person is thinking of her private life, thinking of things going around the house.

No. 22 — **A Military:** The False Person is setting up a battle plan.

No. 23 — **The Court:** The dishonest person thinks about the issues of things; how she can manipulate law to her advantage.

No. 24 — **The Thievery:** The False Person is a thief; she is thinking of how she can take what she wants; pay extra attention.

No. 25 — **High Honours:** Very clever enemy, she wants the first place, wants the gold medal, and will do whatever it takes to obtain it.

No. 26 — **Big Luck:** The False Person thinks of her luck, about how she had succeeded in her plans.

No. 27 — **Unexpected Money:** The False Person thinks about a contract, about a lucrative deal; she will wrong everybody to get the money.

No. 28 — **Expectation:** The False Person is thinking of a middle-aged woman, thinking about her goals and motives. The dishonest person thinks of the future of things.

No. 29 — **The Prison:** The False Person is thinking of how to escape from where she is.

No. 30 — **Legal Matters:** The dishonest person is using a lawyer to turn the situation to her advantage in this legal dispute.

No. 31 — **Short Illness:** The False Person pretends to be sick; she is using her health condition to manipulate everyone around her.

No. 32 — **Grief and Sorrow:** The False Person pretends to be in a difficult situation, and she plans on how to turn this sad situation to her own advantage.

No. 33 — **Murky Thoughts:** The False Person is in a negative mood, lost in fear; she is the drama queen with a lot of negative thoughts.

No. 34 — **Occupation:** The False Person is planning her work; she may be manipulating her colleagues and boss.

No. 35 — **A Long Road:** The dishonest person plans things in advance; her manipulation can continue for a great amount of time.

No. 36 — **Hope, Big Water:** False hope going on, the False Person thinks of moving to a distant country.

When the following appear at the BOTTOM of
No. 8—False Person

Has Achieved

No. 1 — **Main Male:** The male querent is a dishonest person.

No. 2 — **Main Female:** The female querent is a dishonest person.

No. 3 — **Marriage:** The False Person is a happily married woman; she is in a committed relationship/partnership, achieved positive deals and contracts.

No. 4 — **A Meeting:** The False Person is a very social person, involved in events, gatherings, and get-togethers.

No. 5 — **The Good Lord:** The dishonest person controls an older man.

No. 6 — **The Good Lady:** The dishonest person controls an older woman.

No. 7 — **A Pleasant Letter:** The False Person controls communication; she is acting as a filter, not giving the entire piece.

No. 9 — **A Change:** The False Person is a changed woman; she had been through the whole process, even relocating.

No. 10 — **A Journey:** The dishonest person is a kind of gypsy, always on the road; her work may involve traveling a lot.

No. 11 — **Lot of Money:** The False Person has a financial stability, she sits on money, she may be someone that controls every penny spent.

No. 12 — **A Rich Girl:** The dishonest person controls her daughter, sister, or any young female relative; she may be acting like a spoiled child.

No. 13 — **A Rich Man:** The dishonest person controls her son, brother, or any young male relative; she may be acting like a spoiled child.

No. 14 — **Sad News:** The False Person has a displeasing personality, complains about everything, is often the bearer of bad news.

No. 15 — **Success in Love:** The False Person controls her partner, pretending she is truly in love; uses sex and seduction to obtain what she wants.

No. 16 — **His Thoughts:** The False Person is more of an action woman than someone who plans things in advance; she is more logical than practical.

No. 17 — **A Gift:** The False Person loves to receive; she is wearing a mask; not everything that glitters is gold.

No. 18 — **Small Child:** The dishonest person had achieved new beginning, is a mother to come, can also be someone with a naive or childish personality.

No. 19 — **A Funeral:** The dishonest person closely experienced an ending, a separation, or death.

No. 20 — **The House:** The False Person is the owner of her property; she controls every single member of the family.

No. 21 — **The Living Room:** The False Person is a secretive woman, protecting her privacy and intimacy; very attached to her comfort and will do whatever it takes to keep it.

No. 22 — **A Military:** The False Person is someone who wears a uniform; she likes to give orders, rules her life and business with tenacity.

No. 23 — **The Court:** The dishonest person is in control; she has law on her side.

No. 24 — **The Thievery:** The False Person takes things away; she tends to steal from other people and snatches what she wants.

No. 25 — **High Honours:** The dishonest person is known to be a fraud and a traitor.

No. 26 — **Big Luck:** The False Person has undeserved recognition; she will seduce whomever she needs to obtain fame.

No. 27 — **Unexpected Money:** The False Person is in control of this deal; she increases her income through fraudulent means.

No. 28 — **Expectation:** The dishonest person is very patient; she is alert, paying attention to what is on the horizon.

No. 29 — **The Prison:** The False Person is a solitary person; she is sabotaging her enemies.

No. 30 — **Legal Matters:** The False Person uses legal advice to turn things to her advantage.

No. 31 — **Short Illness:** The False Person is an insomniac and does not enjoy a good health. She may have sexual problems.

No. 32 — **Grief and Sorrow:** The False Person is a depressive, addicted person.

No. 33 — **Murky Thoughts:** The dishonest person always sees the glass half empty; likes to keep herself worrying with dark thoughts.

No. 34 — **Occupation:** The False Person is a hardworking, motivated, ambitious woman.

No. 35 — **A Long Road:** The False Person is very patient in her actions and waits for the perfect time to act.

No. 36 — **Hope, Big Water:** The dishonest person is a gifted one but uses her gift to control and manipulate others. She may have psychic abilities, or some kind of artistic talent.

NO. 9
A CHANGE

Keywords

*Change in General, Movement, Breakthrough,
Relocation, A Step Forward*

When this card appears in a reading, it's a sign that a change is on its way. It can represent a change in circumstances or even be a change of direction in all its forms. The surrounding cards will tell you in what area this change is going to operate.

Mantra: All changes in my life are
of my own creation.

Influence: Neutral

Direction: None

Quick answer: Maybe

Topic card: Relocation and change

Card No. 9—A Change with

No. 1 — **Main Male:** A change for the male querent.

No. 2 — **Main Female:** A change for the female querent.

No. 3 — **Marriage:** A change for the couple, a partnership is on its way, a positive deal or contract is coming.

No. 4 — **A Meeting:** A change in an appointment, a social gathering, an event; a changing group.

No. 5 — **The Good Lord:** A change for the older man, a change for the father, a slow relocation.

No. 6 — **The Good Lady:** A change for the older woman, a change for the mother, a slow relocation.

No. 7 — **A Pleasant Letter:** A change brings up good news; a letter or parcel may be diverted or sent to another address.

No. 8 — **False Person:** A wrong change, wrong direction, wrong relocation.

No. 10 — **A Journey:** Things starts to move, travel plans are changed, relocating to the next town.

No. 11 — **Lot of Money:** A change in your finances; the financial change may be positive or negative depending on the surrounding cards.

No. 12 — **A Rich Girl:** A change or relocation for a daughter, a sister, or any young female relative.

No. 13 — **A Rich Man:** A change or relocation for a son, a brother, or any young male relative.

No. 14 — **Sad News:** A change brings up negative or sad news; a change brings along depression.

No. 15 — **Success in Love:** A positive change, love is on its way, a change in your love life.

No. 16 — **His Thoughts:** Changing thoughts, changing the way of planning things, a mixed feeling.

No. 17 — **A Gift:** Housewarming, a positive change, exchanging gifts, a visitor on its way.

No. 18 — **Small Child:** A new beginning, a new phase, a change happening in the morning hours, a small relocation.

No. 19 — **A Funeral:** An ending, a separation, a change happening in the evening.

No. 20 — **The House:** Moving house, moving to your family town, a change happens in the family, house renovation.

No. 21 — **The Living Room:** An intimate change, moving house or apartment, renovation and redecoration, a change in the family.

No. 22 — **A Military:** New regulation and rule, a change that brings up some sort of stress.

No. 23 — **The Court:** A court date is changed; a testimony is modified; renewed summons.

No. 24 — **The Thievery:** Changes are kept secret; being robbed while relocating; a change brings along some losses.

No. 25 — **High Honours:** Fame and acknowledgment bring changes; a change leads to success; a positive change.

No. 26 — **Big Luck:** Lucky change, happy turn, happy outcome, very positive.

No. 27 — **Unexpected Money:** A change brings money, a financial windfall, well-negotiated contracts pay off, unexpected happy surprise.

No. 28 — **Expectation:** An expected change, patiently waiting for a change, waiting for a move.

No. 29 — **The Prison:** No change happening, transfer to a new jail, a change is blocked.

No. 30 — **Legal Matters:** A lawyer brings change through his expertise; a change in legal matters.

No. 31 — **Short Illness:** A disease or illness brings up life changes; relocating due to health issues.

No. 32 — **Grief and Sorrow:** A change causes pain, an unhappy turn of events, a sad situation.

No. 33 — **Murky Thoughts:** Fear of change, not wanting to move or relocate, depressed about an imminent departure.

No. 34 — **Occupation:** Work involves mobility, change in career, change occurring in the workplace with boss and colleagues.

No. 35 — **A Long Road:** Moving or relocating to a distant destination, patience—things will not happen now.

No. 36 — **Hope, Big Water:** Hoping for a change, uncertain change, a change in your spiritual belief or practice.

A CHANGE CARD
IN A READING

*W*hen someone wants to relocate, I use 9 A Change as my focus; I would know if it is a good decision or something that needs more reflection. I will shuffle and focus on my question, tell the deck what I would like to know, and go through the whole deck until I reach 9 A Change, taking the next three cards to interpret. For instance:

9 A Change + 5 The Good Lord + 14 Sad News + 11 Lot of Money

It means that the landlord would ask for a high rental price.

9 A Change + 15 Success in Love + 17 A Gift + 18 Small Child

It announces that the move in under positive omen and a great deal. Let's see a last one!

9 A Change + 10 A Journey + 36 Hope, Big Water + 1 Main Male

It reveals that the querent is moving to a foreign country or immigrating.

I choose to pick the card after A Change card because I want to see the future. As the change card is not directional, I use left or before as past, right or after as future like when you would read a book, left to right.

A JOURNEY

Keywords

Movement, Locomotion, Trip, Transport, Travel

A Journey card is all about movement, small trips, and means of transportation. I use this card as a key card to represent my car or my inland travel. When this card appears in your reading, it is a sign that things are moving now, and you can expect some sort of change happening soon.

A Journey card can invite you to an inner journey (particularly with 16 His Thoughts), leading to new avenues for you to explore.

Mantra: I am always at the right place with the right person at the right time.

Influence: Neutral

Direction: None

Quick answer: Maybe

Topic card: Transportation and trips

Card No. 10—A Journey with

No. 1 — **Main Male:** The male querent is on a journey.

No. 2 — **Main Female:** The female querent is on a journey.

No. 3 — **Marriage:** Traveling to a wedding, going to an event or a ceremony, going into a committed relationship.

No. 4 — **A Meeting:** Traveling to an appointment, going to a meeting, going to a group.

No. 5 — **The Good Lord:** Going to an elderly man, driving an elder man, traveling with an elderly man, traveling with an elderly person.

No. 6 — **The Good Lady:** Going to an elderly woman, driving an elderly woman, traveling with an elderly woman, traveling with elderly person.

No. 7 — **A Pleasant Letter:** Travel document, driver's license, car registration, insurance policy.

No. 8 — **False Person:** Going to an enemy, driving an enemy, traveling with a traitor.

No. 9 — **A Change:** A new car, things start to move on, travel plans are changed.

No. 11 — **Lot of Money:** An expensive car, expenditure related to your car: reparation/renovation, an expensive trip, travel brings money.

No. 12 — **A Rich Girl:** Traveling with a daughter, a sister, or any young female relative; traveling with younger people.

No. 13 — **A Rich Man:** Traveling with a son, a brother, or any young male relative; traveling with younger people.

No. 14 — **Sad News:** A trip is canceled, a broken car, unable to travel.

No. 15 — **Success in Love:** Romantic trip, a holiday flirtation, a successful trip, a loving and precious car.

No. 16 — **His Thoughts:** Changing thoughts, changing the way of planning things, a mixed feeling.

No. 17 — **A Gift:** Getting a car as a gift, a trip as a gift, a positive and surprising trip.

No. 18 — **Small Child:** Traveling with a baby or young child, traveling during daylight; a new start, a new car.

No. 19 — **A Funeral:** Traveling by night, accident during a trip, a journey of no return, a dead car, unrepairable car.

No. 20 — **The House:** A family trip, a secondary house, traveling with family, on the way to home.

No. 21 — **The Living Room:** A secret travel, a personal trip, going to a see a family member.

No. 22 — **A Military:** Official travel, a safe journey, traffic control.

No. 23 — **The Court:** A visa, an entry permit, going to the court, a legal trip.

No. 24 — **The Thievery:** A clandestine trip, risk of being robbed during this travel, car loss, traveling to a fraud, driving a fraud.

No. 25 — **High Honours:** A successful travel, trip to a ceremony, a graduation, been rewarded or winning a car.

No. 26 — **Big Luck:** Lucky change, happy turn, happy outcome, very positive.

No. 27 — **Unexpected Money:** A trip brings some money, traveling for a negotiation, unexpected happy journey, traveling with a middle-aged woman.

No. 28 — **Expectation:** An expected travel, a departure is awaited, traveling with a middle-aged woman.

No. 29 — **The Prison:** Traveling to a prison; a journey leads to imprisonment.

No. 30 — **Legal Matters:** Going to an expert; car seizure, a complaint related to a travel or a car.

No. 31 — **Short Illness:** Car sickness, going to a sick person, not feeling good during a trip.

No. 32 — **Grief and Sorrow:** A trip causes pain, a car brings a lot of worries, a painful travel.

No. 33 — **Murky Thoughts:** Fear of driving, not wanting to travel, depressed about an imminent departure.

No. 34 — **Occupation:** Work involves mobility; driving to work, car salesman, working in the tourism industry.

No. 35 — **A Long Road:** Traveling to a foreign country; a long travel, a long distance, a faraway place.

No. 36 — **Hope, Big Water:** Great hopes on a journey, a cruise, a meditation journey, a spiritual journey.

A JOURNEY CARD
IN A READING

*W*hen I conduct a mediumship reading, 10 A Journey is an important one as it refers to crossing over, the other dimension, and the other side, particularly when it appears next to 19 A Funeral or 36 Hope, Big Water. Let me give you some examples of messages from above:

10 A Journey + 19 A Funeral + 5 The Good Lord

Grandpa is saying "Hello" from heaven.

12 A Rich Girl + 10 A Journey + 3 Marriage

A young female is stepping forward; Spirit is acknowledging a wedding or a ceremony.

22 A Military + 10 A Journey + 35 A Long Road

A person in uniform, who is not always present or has been on a mission far away, is saying hello!

As you can see, these cards are not only for predictions and fortune telling; you can also get spiritual messages. The more you practice with them, the more they will unveil their secrets to you.

LOT OF MONEY

Keywords
Gain, Plenty, Money, a Large Sum, Income, Inheritance, Lottery Prize

It's all about money!

No. 11 Lot of Money is a card that relates to the financial situation of the questioner and their further development. This card talks about money in great amounts; it can be money gained through gambling and ensures that all kinds of transactions are successful.

With negative cards around, the gain can change into loss, or spending money on futile things.

Mantra: I am friend of money.

Influence: Positive

Direction: None

Quick answer: Yes

Topic card: Money

Card No. 11—Lot of Money with

No. 1 — **Main Male:** Money for the male querent.

No. 2 — **Main Female:** Money for the female querent.

No. 3 — **Marriage:** Money from a couple, through a contract, a commitment, a deal.

No. 4 — **A Meeting:** Appointment with a bank; a group of investors, dividends, shares of a society.

No. 5 — **The Good Lord:** Money for the elder man; money for a father, grandfather; an inheritance.

No. 6 — **The Good Lady:** Money for the elder woman; money for a mother, grandmother; an inheritance.

No. 7 — **A Pleasant Letter:** A check, a pay slip, good news about money, a money transfer.

No. 8 — **False Person:** A fraud, dirty money, money obtained unlawfully or immorally.

No. 9 — **A Change:** Money coming in; money brings changes; a raise, an increase in income.

No. 10 — **A Journey:** An expensive car, expenditure related to your car: reparation/renovation, an expensive trip, travel brings money.

No. 12 — **A Rich Girl:** Well-stocked bank accounts, valuable stock exchange, a rich young woman, someone really good with money.

No. 13 — **A Rich Man:** Well-stocked bank accounts, valuable stock exchange, a rich young man, someone really good with money.

No. 14 — **Sad News:** Money causes worries, financial burden, bills to pay, an unfortunate investment.

No. 15 — **Success in Love:** Significant romantic relationship, relationship based upon money, a financial success.

No. 16 — **His Thoughts:** Creating a financial plan; money causes a lot of reflection.

No. 17 — **A Gift:** A donation, a gift of money, an inheritance, surprising sum of money.

No. 18 — **Small Child:** An inheritance, new source of income, new financial transaction.

No. 19 — **A Funeral:** An inheritance, ruin, money spent for a funeral, money from life insurance.

No. 20 — **The House:** Money for the family, an inheritance, purchasing a house, loan and mortgage.

No. 21 — **The Living Room:** Money for the family, an inheritance, purchasing an apartment, a condominium, loan and mortgage.

No. 22 — **A Military:** Money from an authority, secure transaction, safe investment.

No. 23 — **The Court:** Money from an authority, a tax refund, paying for a law trial.

No. 24 — **The Thievery:** Money is stolen, money is lost, a fraud.

No. 25 — **High Honours:** A bonus, a raise, a valuable prize, raising your standards.

No. 26 — **Big Luck:** Wealth, fortune, prosperity; money is your best friend.

No. 27 — **Unexpected Money:** Unexpected sum of money, money for a middle-aged woman, payment comes unexpectedly.

No. 28 — **Expectation:** A large sum of money is expected, a rich middle-aged woman.

No. 29 — **The Prison:** Tax evasion, money blocked, fee from a hospital or sanatorium costs much.

No. 30 — **Legal Matters:** Paying for a lawyer, financial advisor, fighting for money, money may cause some argument.

No. 31 — **Short Illness:** Expensive healthcare; money may cause some illness.

No. 32 — **Grief and Sorrow:** Money brings grief; big money problem, major financial obstacles.

No. 33 — **Murky Thoughts:** Existential fear, fear of money, negative thoughts about money, feeling undeserving.

No. 34 — **Occupation:** Money through work, a raise in salary, good salary, working with money, investors.

No. 35 — **A Long Road:** Long-term investment, money on the distance, money out of reach.

No. 36 — **Hope, Big Water:** Money comes from abroad, investing in your spirituality, good intuition on money.

If you want money more than anything, you'll be bought and sold your whole life.

—RUMI

NO. 12
A RICH GIRL

Keywords

Young Female, Daughter, Sister, Artist, Carefree,
Joyous, Beauty, Grace

$\mathcal{T}$his card represents a precious young female in your surroundings, someone who is carefree and slightly immature in her behaviors. She had always known comfort and is privileged.

A Rich Girl is joyous, very talented, has a carefree existence. She can sometimes be selfish, lacking maturity, too spontaneous, and she does and says things that she later regrets. She needs to grow up, and hopefully positive cards will help her in this task.

Mantra: I live my life with joy and happiness.

Influence: Positive

Direction: Facing right

Quick answer: Yes

Topic card: Luxury and talent

The Past

No. 1 — **Main Male:** Dispute and argument with the young lady's father, a generation gap, father and daughter refusing to see each other.

No. 2 — **Main Female:** Dispute and argument with the young lady's mother; a generation gap.

No. 3 — **Marriage:** The younger lady was married, committed in a past relationship; the younger woman has turned the page.

No. 4 — **A Meeting:** The young woman was in a meeting, an event has taken place, taking distance from a group of people, leaving a meet-up.

No. 5 — **The Good Lord:** Turning away from an elder man, contact with an elder is difficult, grandfather/grandchild relationship issues.

No. 6 — **The Good Lady:** Turning away from an elder man, contact with an elder is difficult, grandmother/grandchild relationship issues.

No. 7 — **A Pleasant Letter:** A message received, past communication, past conversation.

No. 8 — **False Person:** Away from an enemy, rival; cunning, dangerous person who is backstabbing the younger female.

No. 9 — **A Change:** A recent change, recent move or relocation, a planned occurrence.

No. 10 — **A Journey:** The young female has left behind her a person, place, or situation; a recent travel; a planned trip didn't turn out the way it was hoped.

No. 11 — **Lot of Money:** Financial crisis, money goes, the young female does not see this opportunity, the young female turns back to a positive transaction.

No. 13 — **A Rich Man:** Disputes with a brother or any young male relative, turning back to a young male, ending with an ex-lover.

No. 14 — **Sad News:** Negative or sad news received, depression is over, letting go of sadness.

No. 15 — **Success in Love:** The younger female was in love, a love affair is over, a positive relationship from the past.

No. 16 — **His Thoughts:** The rich girl is no more preoccupied; she has been through a period of reflection, and a solution had been found.

No. 17 — **A Gift:** External circumstances had brought joy, the young female was visited, she received a gift.

No. 18 — **Small Child:** Abortion, miscarriage; children are a source of worry; not the right time for a new beginning.

No. 19 — **A Funeral:** The young female lost someone, something is now buried, a break free, being through a transformation, being through grief.

No. 20 — **The House:** A luxurious house, a young neighbor or neighborhood, a girl from a good family.

No. 21 — **The Living Room:** A luxurious apartment, a young neighbor, a daughter leaving with her parents.

No. 22 — **A Military:** An ex-boyfriend in uniform, the younger female rejected domination, she lives on her own rules.

No. 23 — **The Court:** Official matters are regulated; the young female was wrong.

No. 24 — **The Thievery:** Something or someone was taken away from the rich girl and the thief escaped.

No. 25 — **High Honours:** A young woman with high education; a young female with good reputation is acknowledged for her talents.

No. 26 — **Big Luck:** The rich girl is a fortunate one, everything she does is a success, she has the Midas touch.

No. 27 — **Unexpected Money:** The rich girl concluded a contract, she had sold her art and talent, received an unexpected sum of money.

No. 28 — **Expectation:** Patience is over; the rich girl had met a middle-aged woman. Prosperity and luxury are expected.

No. 29 — **The Prison:** The woman was lonely; experience a lack of freedom, being lonely; with other cards related to health, she could have been admitted to a hospital for treatment.

No. 30 — **Legal Matters:** The rich girl was wrong; the lawyer is not in her favor.

No. 31 — **Short Illness:** Recovering from a short illness, health impairment.

No. 32 — **Grief and Sorrow:** Gone through difficult times, out of a depression, healing from addiction.

No. 33 — **Murky Thoughts:** Disenchantment, leaving the drama queen behind.

No. 34 — **Occupation:** Distancing oneself from work or the young female had been working hard lately.

No. 35 — **A Long Road:** Was away to a distant destination, had shown a lot of patience, was out of patience.

No. 36 — **Hope, Big Water:** The rich girl lost hope, coming from abroad to a foreign land, feeling hopeful, a dream had manifested into reality.

When the following appear on the RIGHT of
No. 12—A Rich Girl

The Future

No. 1 — **Main Male:** Harmonious relationship, a talented young lady for the querent, a father, the daughter makes peace.

No. 2 — **Main Female:** Disputes and argument with the young lady's mother, a generation gap, mother-and-daughter issue, the rich girl will meet the female querent in the future.

No. 3 — **Marriage:** The younger female is looking forward to a commitment, a partnership is on its way, a positive deal or contract.

No. 4 — **A Meeting:** An appointment, a social gathering, an event, meeting a group, a privileged group.

No. 5 — **The Good Lord:** Dealing with an older man, a supportive friend, a grandfather, a protector.

No. 6 — **The Good Lady:** Dealing with an older woman, supportive female friend, a grandmother, a godmother.

No. 7 — **A Pleasant Letter:** Good news, news to come, positive correspondence, positive phone calls.

No. 8 — **False Person:** Enemy, rival; cunning, dangerous person; pay attention as she is there only for the luxury and advantages!

No. 9 — **A Change:** A change is imminent, the rich girl will move or relocate, a planned change will succeed.

No. 10 — **A Journey:** Planned changes will succeed, a positive trip, embarking for a journey, first-class travel.

No. 11 — **Lot of Money:** Financial stability, money comes, wealth and abundance, luxury, more money for the privileged young lady.

No. 13 — **A Rich Man:** Interaction with a brother or any young male relative, closeness with a young male, a young lover.

No. 14 — **Sad News:** Receiving negative or sad news, a depressed mood, dealing with some bad news.

No. 15 — **Success in Love:** The rich girl falls in love; a love affair, a happy and positive love life.

No. 16 — **His Thoughts:** The rich girl is preoccupied; she is very thoughtful and a lot is going on in his mind.

No. 17 — **A Gift:** External circumstances bring joy, a gift, a pleasant visit, a luxurious gift.

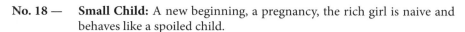

No. 18 — **Small Child:** A new beginning, a pregnancy, the rich girl is naive and behaves like a spoiled child.

No. 19 — **A Funeral:** An ending, a separation, assisting with a funeral, a luxurious funeral.

No. 20 — **The House:** Buying a property; a cozy woman, a family house, a luxurious house.

No. 21 — **The Living Room:** The rich girl feels at home, the rich girl's personal space, a luxurious apartment.

No. 22 — **A Military:** Official matters are on the agenda, encountering someone wearing a uniform, a rich girl with a man in uniform.

No. 23 — **The Court:** A final decision, justice triumphs, official matter will be regulated, the rich girl is trustworthy.

No. 24 — **The Thievery:** Recovering a lost object, the thief is caught, a luxurious item is stolen.

No. 25 — **High Honours:** The rich girl is successful, she receives recognition, a promotion may be on the horizon.

No. 26 — **Big Luck:** A privileged young lady; she can expect happy outcome and a lot of success in her ventures.

No. 27 — **Unexpected Money:** A windfall, well-negotiated contracts are now paying off, unexpected happy surprise; she will be able to sell her art and talents.

No. 28 — **Expectation:** The rich girl is patient and has strong desires; the next card will say what kind of expectation she has.

No. 29 — **The Prison:** The rich girl is restricted in her actions, alone, locked away, correctional facility, standstill, stagnation. A treatment in a hospital.

No. 30 — **Legal Matters:** Seeing a lawyer, seeking expertise, dealing with legal matters; she perfectly knows her rights.

No. 31 — **Short Illness:** Weak health condition, fever, small infection, light depression, need to rest, need to sleep.

No. 32 — **Grief and Sorrow:** A difficult time to come, problems and difficulties pile up in front of the younger female, a pattern, a depression, addicted to luxury.

No. 33 — **Murky Thoughts:** Negative mood, lost in fear, drama queen, negative thinking.

No. 34 — **Occupation:** Hardworking, motivated, talented ambitious young woman; a job offer, a job in the luxury industry.

No. 35 — **A Long Road:** Traveling to a distant destination, patience—things will not happen now.

No. 36 — **Hope, Big Water:** Traveling abroad, traveling in first class, crossing waters; the event will happen in a foreign land; feeling hopeful.

When the following appear on the TOP of
No. 12—A Rich Girl

On the Mind

No. 1 — **Main Male:** The rich girl thinks of a particular man: her husband, her partner, a significant man in her life.

No. 2 — **Main Female:** The rich girl thinks of a particular woman: her mother, her partner, a significant woman in her life.

No. 3 — **Marriage:** The rich girl dreams of a harmonious relationship, thinking about a future partnership or deal.

No. 4 — **A Meeting:** She thinks of an appointment, a social gathering, an event, meeting a group.

No. 5 — **The Good Lord:** The young female thinks about an older man, a supportive friend, a grandfather.

No. 6 — **The Good Lady:** The young female thinks about an older woman, supportive female friend, a grandmother.

No. 7 — **A Pleasant Letter:** The rich girl longs for better communication, thinking about a message or a correspondence.

No. 8 — **False Person:** Thinking of an enemy, a rival; a cunning, dangerous person who likes luxury.

No. 9 — **A Change:** Thinking about a change, the rich girl thinks about a move or a relocation; thinking about a change.

No. 10 — **A Journey:** Thinking about a planned change, about a trip. Longing for a particular destination.

No. 11 — **Lot of Money:** The rich girl thinks about her financial stability, constantly thinking about her finances. Money and luxury are very important for the rich girl.

No. 13 — **A Rich Man:** Thinking of a brother or any young male relative; thinking of a young lover.

No. 14 — **Sad News:** Sorrowful thoughts, fear of bad news, negative thoughts, cupidity.

No. 15 — **Success in Love:** The young female thinks about success, thinking about her love life, thinks about friendship.

No. 16 — **His Thoughts:** The rich girl is thinking a lot; she is making plans.

No. 17 — **A Gift:** The young female thinks about a gift, thoughts of a pleasant visit.

No. 18 — **Small Child:** The young female thinks of a new beginning; innocent thoughts, naive thoughts, planning something new, thinking of a baby.

No. 19 — **A Funeral:** Thinking of an ending, of a separation; thinking of a funeral.

No. 20 — **The House:** Thinking about a property, of constructing something.

No. 21 — **The Living Room:** Thinking of her private life, thinking about things going on around the house, thinking of an apartment.

No. 22 — **A Military:** The young female has a feeling of being controlled, thinking about a strategy, making up a battle plan.

No. 23 — **The Court:** Thinking of a legal issue, thinking about an important decision, thinking of a deadline.

No. 24 — **The Thievery:** Thinking of a lost object, reviewing a loss; the rich girl thinks about taking something away.

No. 25 — **High Honours:** The rich girl thinks about studying; she is intelligent and aware of her talents and capacities.

No. 26 — **Big Luck:** The rich girl thinks of her luck, of the various doors opening before her.

No. 27 — **Unexpected Money:** The querent thinks about a contract, about a lucrative deal; she may also be worried by her finances.

No. 28 — **Expectation:** The young female thinks about a middle-aged woman; thinking about her goals and motives, thinking about the future of things.

No. 29 — **The Prison:** The rich girl is thinking about her loneliness, dreaming of freedom.

No. 30 — **Legal Matters:** The young female is considering the help of a lawyer, considering legal dispute.

No. 31 — **Short Illness:** Thinking about his weak health condition, insomnia; the rich girl should uplift her thought in this situation.

No. 32 — **Grief and Sorrow:** Thinking of a difficult time to come; problems and difficulties are piling up; facing a depression even an addiction.

No. 33 — **Murky Thoughts:** The young female is in a negative mood; lost in fear, drama queen, negative thinking.

No. 34 — **Occupation:** Preoccupied by her work; the rich girl's work involves a lot of her logic and intelligence.

No. 35 — **A Long Road:** Thinking of a distant destination, the rich girl plans things in advance.

No. 36 — **Hope, Big Water:** The young female is fascinated by foreign culture, needs to ground herself.

When the following appear at the BOTTOM of
No. 12—A Rich Girl

Has Achieved

No. 1 — **Main Male:** The rich girl has a partner, a husband; has someone significant in her life.

No. 2 — **Main Female:** The rich girl has a partner, has someone significant in her life.

No. 3 — **Marriage:** The rich girl is a happily married woman; she is in a committed relationship/partnership, achieved positive deals and contracts.

No. 4 — **A Meeting:** The young female is a very social person; involved in events, gatherings, and get-togethers.

No. 5 — **The Good Lord:** Is a good person, supportive of her friend.

No. 6 — **The Good Lady:** Is a good person, supportive of her friend.

No. 7 — **A Pleasant Letter:** Has a pleasant personality, communicates a lot with others, is often the bearer of good news.

No. 8 — **False Person:** The rich girl may be sabotaging herself; she is her own rival. The young female has a cunning personality, needs to change the way she behaves in life.

No. 9 — **A Change:** The young female is a changed woman; she had been through a whole process, even relocating.

No. 10 — **A Journey:** The rich girl is a kind of gypsy, always; her work may involve traveling a lot.

No. 11 — **Lot of Money:** The younger female has financial stability; she sits on money; she may be someone who controls every penny spent. The young female is rich.

No. 13 — **A Rich Man:** The rich girl is close to her brother or any young male relative; she may be acting like a spoiled child; the rich girl has a lover.

No. 14 — **Sad News:** The rich girl has a displeasing personality, complains about everything, is often the bearer of bad news.

No. 15 — **Success in Love:** The rich girl is a loyal partner, tied to her intention, respectful of her relationship, can be trusted 100%.

No. 16 — **His Thoughts:** The younger female is more of an action girl than someone who plans things in advance; she is more logical than practical.

No. 17 — **A Gift:** Loves to give and receive, has a surprising personality and is known to be a gift to others, is a rich girl, is generous.

No. 18 —   **Small Child:** The young female achieved a new beginning, is a mother to come, can also be someone with a naive personality, is a spoiled child.

No. 19 —   **A Funeral:** The rich girl closely experienced an ending, a separation, or death.

No. 20 —   **The House:** The young female is the owner of her property; a cozy woman; she is a family girl, tied to family values.

No. 21 —   **The Living Room:** Is a secretive woman, protecting her privacy and intimacy, very attached to her home; the rich girl has an apartment.

No. 22 —   **A Military:** The young female is someone who wears a uniform; she likes discipline and order, rules her life and business with righteousness.

No. 23 —   **The Court:** High minded, the rich girl is someone who has principles; she always honors deadlines.

No. 24 —   **The Thievery:** The rich girl is someone that takes things away, she tends to steal from other people and snatch what she wants, she had built her fortune with dirty money.

No. 25 —   **High Honours:** The rich girl is acknowledged and enjoys a good reputation and is seen as a leader; she is highly educated.

No. 26 —   **Big Luck:** The rich girl is a lucky woman; she knows it and uses her luck in all of her ventures.

No. 27 —   **Unexpected Money:** The rich girl deals well with her contract; her income is constantly increasing.

No. 28 —   **Expectation:** Patience is a virtue for our rich girl; she is always alert, paying attention to what is on the horizon.

No. 29 —   **The Prison:** The rich girl is solitary; she may be sabotaging herself; the rich girl is in a golden cage.

No. 30 —   **Legal Matters:** The rich girl is interested in counsel and advice and uses her wisdom to restore peace and happiness; the rich girl is a lawyer.

No. 31 —   **Short Illness:** She is an insomniac and does not enjoy good health. She may have sexual problems.

No. 32 —   **Grief and Sorrow:** The rich girl is a depressive, addicted person.

No. 33 —   **Murky Thoughts:** Always sees the glass half empty, likes to keep herself worrying with dark thoughts.

No. 34 —   **Occupation:** Hardworking, motivated, ambitious; a talented woman.

No. 35 —   **A Long Road:** The rich girl is patient in her action, waits for the perfect time to act.

No. 36 —   **Hope, Big Water:** The rich girl is a gifted one; she may have psychic abilities or some kind of artistic talent.

NO. 13
A RICH MAN

Keywords

Young Male, Son, Brother, Artist, Carefree, Joyous,
Handsome, Well Groomed

This card represents a handsome young male in your surroundings—someone who is carefree, slightly immature in his attitude. He has always known comfort—a "Casanova" type of person, a joyous gentleman.

A Rich Man is talented and excels in financial transactions; he is the perfect ally if you need a loan or an investor. Everything he does is a success.

Mantra: I live my life with joy and happiness.

Influence: Positive

Direction: Facing Left

Quick answer: Yes

Topic card: Luxury and talent

When the following appear on the LEFT of
No. 13—A Rich Man

The Future

No. 1 — **Main Male:** Dispute and argument with the querent, a generation gap, father-and-son issue; the rich man will meet the male querent in the future.

No. 2 — **Main Female:** Harmonious relationship, a talented young man for the female querent. The Rich Man will meet the female querent in the future.

No. 3 — **Marriage:** The younger male is looking forward to a commitment, a partnership is on its way, a positive deal or contract.

No. 4 — **A Meeting:** The younger male goes to an appointment, a social gathering, an event, meeting a group, a privileged group.

No. 5 — **The Good Lord:** The younger male deals with an older man, a supportive friend, a grandfather.

No. 6 — **The Good Lady:** The younger male deals with an older woman, a supportive female friend, a grandmother.

No. 7 — **A Pleasant Letter:** The younger male receives good news, a positive correspondence, positive phone calls.

No. 8 — **False Person:** Enemy to the younger male, rival; cunning, dangerous person, he/she is there only for the luxury and the advantages!

No. 9 — **A Change:** A change is imminent, the Rich Man will move or relocate, a planned change will succeed.

No. 10 — **A Journey:** The younger male goes on a positive trip, embarking on a journey, first-class travel.

No. 11 — **Lot of Money:** Financial stability, money comes, wealth and abundance, luxury, more money for the privileged young man.

No. 12 — **A Rich Girl:** Interaction with a sister or any young female relative, closeness with a young female, a young lover.

No. 14 — **Sad News:** The younger male receives negative news; he is in a depressed mood, dealing with some bad news.

No. 15 — **Success in Love:** The rich young man falls in love; love affair, a happy and positive love life.

No. 16 — **His Thoughts:** The rich young man is preoccupied, very thoughtful; a lot is going on in his mind.

No. 17 — **A Gift:** External circumstances bring joy to the Rich Man; a gift, a pleasant visit, a luxurious gift.

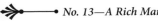

No. 18 — **Small Child:** A new beginning, a pregnancy; the Rich Man is naive and is a spoiled child.

No. 19 — **A Funeral:** An ending, a separation for the younger man, assisting with a funeral, a luxurious funeral.

No. 20 — **The House:** The younger male buys a property; a cozy man, a family house, a luxurious house.

No. 21 — **The Living Room:** The Rich Man feels at home; the Rich Man's personal space, a luxurious apartment.

No. 22 — **A Military:** Official matters are on the agenda for the young man, encountering some wearing a uniform, a rich man with a man in uniform.

No. 23 — **The Court:** A final decision, justice is in favor of the Rich Man; official matter will be regulated; the rich man is trustworthy.

No. 24 — **The Thievery:** The younger male recovers a lost object, the thief is caught, a luxurious item is stolen.

No. 25 — **High Honours:** The Rich Man is successful; he receives recognition; a promotion is on the horizon.

No. 26 — **Big Luck:** A privileged young man, he can expect happy outcome and a lot of success in his ventures.

No. 27 — **Unexpected Money:** A windfall for the younger man, contracts well negotiated are now paying off, unexpected happy surprise, he will be able to sell his art and talent.

No. 28 — **Expectation:** The Rich Man is patient and has strong desires; the next card will say what kind of expectation he has.

No. 29 — **The Prison:** The Rich Man is restricted in his actions; lonely, locked away, correctional facility, standstill, stagnation, treatment in a hospital.

No. 30 — **Legal Matters:** The younger male sees a lawyer, seeking expertise dealing with legal matters; he knows his rights perfectly.

No. 31 — **Short Illness:** Weak health condition, fever, small infection, light depression for the younger man. Need to rest, need to sleep.

No. 32 — **Grief and Sorrow:** A difficult time to come for the younger male; problems and difficulties pile up in front of him. A pattern, a depression, addicted to luxury.

No. 33 — **Murky Thoughts:** The younger male is in a negative mood, lost in fear, drama queen, negative thinking.

No. 34 — **Occupation:** Hardworking, motivated, talented ambitious young man. A job offer, a job in the luxury industry.

No. 35 — **A Long Road:** The younger male travels to a distant destination; patience—things will not happen now.

No. 36 — **Hope, Big Water:** The younger male is traveling abroad, traveling in first class, crossing waters; predicted event will happen in a foreign land; feeling hopeful.

When the following appear on the RIGHT of
No. 13—A Rich Man

The Past

No. 1 — **Main Male:** Disputes and argument with the young man's father, a generation gap; the Rich Man refuses to see his father.

No. 2 — **Main Female:** Disputes and arguments with the young man's mother, a generation gap.

No. 3 — **Marriage:** The younger man was married, committed in a past relationship. The younger man had turned the page.

No. 4 — **A Meeting:** The young man was in a meeting; an event had taken place. The younger male takes his distance with a group of people; he left the meet-up.

No. 5 — **The Good Lord:** The younger male turned away from an elder man, contact with an elder is difficult; grandfather/grandchild relationship issue.

No. 6 — **The Good Lady:** The younger male turned away from an elder man, contact with an elder is difficult; grandmother/grandchild relationship issue.

No. 7 — **A Pleasant Letter:** The younger male received a message; past communication, past conversation.

No. 8 — **False Person:** The younger male is away from an enemy, rival, and cunning, dangerous person.

No. 9 — **A Change:** The younger male had been through a recent change, a recent move or relocation; something planned happened.

No. 10 — **A Journey:** The young male had left a person, place, or situation. A recent travel, a planned trip didn't turn out the way it was hoped.

No. 11 — **Lot of Money:** Financial crisis, money goes, the young male does not see this opportunity, the younger male turns his back to a positive transaction.

No. 13 — **A Rich Girl:** The younger male argued with a sister or any young female relative; turning his back to a young female, ending with an ex-lover.

No. 14 —   **Sad News:** Negative or sad news received, depression is over, letting go of sadness.

No. 15 —   **Success in Love:** The younger male was in love, love affair is over; a positive relationship from the past.

No. 16 —   **His Thoughts:** The Rich Man is no longer preoccupied; he has been through a period of reflection; solution had been found.

No. 17 —   **A Gift:** External circumstances have brought joy, the young male was visited, a gift was received.

No. 18 —   **Small Child:** Abortion, miscarriage; children are a source of worry for the younger male; not the right time for a new beginning.

No. 19 —   **A Funeral:** The young male lost someone, something is now buried, a break free. Being through a transformation, being through grief.

No. 20 —   **The House:** A luxurious house, a young neighbor, a young man comes from a good family.

No. 21 —   **The Living Room:** A luxurious apartment, a young neighbor, a son who was living with his parents.

No. 22 —   **A Military:** An ex-boyfriend in uniform, the younger male rejected domination, he lives on his own rules.

No. 23 —   **The Court:** Official matters were regulated; the young male was wronged.

No. 24 —   **The Thievery:** Something or someone was taken away from the Rich Man and the thief escaped.

No. 25 —   **High Honours:** A young man with high education, a young male with good reputation, was acknowledged for his talents.

No. 26 —   **Big Luck:** The Rich Man was fortunate, credited with many successful transactions.

No. 27 —   **Unexpected Money:** The Rich Man concluded a contract; he has sold his art and talent and received an unexpected sum of money.

No. 28 —   **Expectation:** Patience is over, the Rich Man had met a middle-aged woman, prosperity and luxury are expected.

No. 29 —   **The Prison:** The Rich Man was lonely, experiencing a lack of freedom; with other cards related to health, he could have been admitted to a hospital for treatment.

No. 30 —   **Legal Matters:** The rich man was wronged; the law was not in his favor.

No. 31 —   **Short Illness:** The younger male recovered from a short illness, health impairment.

No. 32 —   **Grief and Sorrow:** The younger male has gone through a difficult time; out of a depression, healed from addiction.

No. 33 —   **Murky Thoughts:** Disenchantment, leaving the drama queen behind.

No. 34 — **Occupation:** The younger male distanced himself from work or has been working hard lately.

No. 35 — **A Long Road:** The younger male was away to a distant destination; he has shown a lot of patience and may be out of patience now.

No. 36 — **Hope, Big Water:** The rich man lost hope, coming from abroad to a foreign land, feeling hopeful, a dream has manifested into reality.

When the following appear on the TOP of
No. 13—A Rich Man

On the Mind

No. 1 — **Main Male:** The rich man is thinking of a particular man: his father, his partner, a significant man in his life.

No. 2 — **Main Female:** The rich man is thinking of a particular woman: his mother, his partner, a significant woman in his life.

No. 3 — **Marriage:** The rich man dreams of a harmonious relationship, thinking about a future partnership or deal.

No. 4 — **A Meeting:** The younger male is thinking of an appointment, a social gathering, an event, meeting a group.

No. 5 — **The Good Lord:** The younger male is thinking about an older man, a supportive friend, a grandfather.

No. 6 — **The Good Lady:** The younger male is thinking about an older woman, a supportive female friend, a grandmother.

No. 7 — **A Pleasant Letter:** The rich man longs for better communication, is thinking about a message or a correspondence.

No. 8 — **False Person:** The younger male is thinking of an enemy, a rival; a cunning, dangerous person who likes luxury.

No. 9 — **A Change:** Thinking about a change, the rich man is thinking about a move or a relocation.

No. 10 — **A Journey:** The younger male is thinking about a planned change, about a trip. Longing for a particular destination.

No. 11 — **Lot of Money:** The rich man is thinking of his financial stability, constantly thinking about his finances; money and luxury are very important for the rich man.

No. 12 — **A Rich Girl:** The younger male is thinking of a sister or any young female relative; thinking of a young lover.

No. 14 —   **Sad News:** The younger male has sorrowful thoughts, fear of bad news, negative thoughts, cupidity.

No. 15 —   **Success in Love:** The younger male is thinking of his success; thinking about his love life and friendship.

No. 16 —   **His Thoughts:** The rich man is thinking a lot; he is making plans.

No. 17 —   **A Gift:** The younger male is thinking of a gift; thoughts of a pleasant visit.

No. 18 —   **Small Child:** The younger male is thinking of a new beginning, has innocent or naive thoughts, is planning something new, is thinking of a baby.

No. 19 —   **A Funeral:** The younger male is thinking of an ending, of a separation, of a funeral.

No. 20 —   **The House:** The younger male is thinking of a property, of constructing something.

No. 21 —   **The Living Room:** The younger male is thinking of his private life, thinking about things going around the house, thinking of an apartment.

No. 22 —   **A Military:** The younger male has a feeling of being controlled, thinking about a strategy, making up a battle plan.

No. 23 —   **The Court:** The younger male is thinking of a legal issue, thinking about an important decision, thinking about a deadline.

No. 24 —   **The Thievery:** The younger male is thinking of a lost object, he is reviewing a loss; the rich man thought of taking something away.

No. 25 —   **High Honours:** The rich man thinks about studying; he is intelligent and aware of his talents and capacities.

No. 26 —   **Big Luck:** The rich man thinks of his luck, of the various doors opening before him.

No. 27 —   **Unexpected Money:** The younger male is thinking about a contract, about a lucrative deal; he may also be worried by his finances.

No. 28 —   **Expectation:** The younger male is thinking about a middle-aged woman, thinking about his goals and motives, thinking about the future of things.

No. 29 —   **The Prison:** The rich man is thinking about his loneliness; he dreams of freedom.

No. 30 —   **Legal Matters:** The younger male is considering the help of a lawyer, considering legal disputes.

No. 31 —   **Short Illness:** The younger male is thinking about his weak health condition; he suffers insomnia. The rich man should uplift his thoughts in this situation.

No. 32 —   **Grief and Sorrow:** The younger male is thinking of a difficult time to come, of problems and difficulties that are piling up; he is facing a depression—even an addiction.

No. 33 —	**Murky Thoughts:** The younger male is in a negative mood; lost in fear, drama queen, has a negative thinking pattern.
No. 34 —	**Occupation:** The younger male is preoccupied by his work; the rich man's work involves a lot of his logic and intelligence.
No. 35 —	**A Long Road:** The younger male is thinking of a distant destination; the rich man plans things in advance.
No. 36 —	**Hope, Big Water:** The younger male is fascinated by foreign culture. He needs to ground himself.

When the following appear at the BOTTOM of
No. 13—A Rich Man

Has Achieved

No. 1 —	**Main Male:** The rich man has a partner, has someone significant in his life.
No. 2 —	**Main Female:** The rich female has a partner, has someone significant in her life.
No. 3 —	**Marriage:** The rich man is a happily married man, he is in a committed relationship/partnership, he achieved positive deals and contracts.
No. 4 —	**A Meeting:** The younger male is a very social person, involved in events, gatherings, and get-togethers.
No. 5 —	**The Good Lord:** The younger male is a good person, supportive of his friend.
No. 6 —	**The Good Lady:** The younger male is thinking of a good person, supportive of his friend.
No. 7 —	**A Pleasant Letter:** The younger male has a pleasant personality, communicates a lot with others, is often the bearer of good news.
No. 8 —	**False Person:** The rich man may be sabotaging himself; he is his own rival. He has a cunning personality, needs to change the way he behaves in life.
No. 9 —	**A Change:** The young man is a changed man; he had been through a whole process. The younger male has relocated.
No. 10 —	**A Journey:** The rich man is a kind of gypsy, always on the road; his work may involve a lot of traveling.
No. 11 —	**Lot of Money:** The younger male has financial stability; he has a lot of resources; he may be someone who controls every penny spent.

No. 12 — **A Rich Girl:** The younger male is close to his sister or with a young female relative. He acts as a spoiled child as well; the rich man has a young lover.

No. 14 — **Sad News:** The rich man has a displeasing personality, complains about everything, is often the bearer of bad news.

No. 15 — **Success in Love:** The rich man is a loyal partner; he is tied to his intention and respectful of his relationship, can be trusted 100%.

No. 16 — **His Thoughts:** The younger male is thinking more of an action man than someone who plans things in advance; he is more logical than practical.

No. 17 — **A Gift:** The younger male loves to give and receive, with a surprising personality; he is known to be a gift to others; the rich man is generous.

No. 18 — **Small Child:** The younger male has achieved a new beginning, is a father to come, can be someone with a naive personality acting like a spoiled child.

No. 19 — **A Funeral:** The rich man closely experienced an ending, a separation, or death.

No. 20 — **The House:** The younger male is the owner of her property; a cozy man; he is a family guy and is tied to family values.

No. 21 — **The Living Room:** The younger male is a secretive man, protects his privacy and intimacy, very attached to his home; the rich man has an apartment.

No. 22 — **A Military:** The younger male is someone who wears a uniform; he likes discipline and order, rules his life and business with righteousness.

No. 23 — **The Court:** High minded, the rich man is someone who has principles; he always honors his deadlines.

No. 24 — **The Thievery:** The rich man is someone who takes things away; he tends to steal from other people and snatches what he wants. He has built his fortune with dirty money.

No. 25 — **High Honours:** The rich man is acknowledged, enjoys a good reputation, is seen as a leader, is highly educated.

No. 26 — **Big Luck:** The rich man is a lucky man; he knows it and uses his luck in all of his ventures.

No. 27 — **Unexpected Money:** The rich man is someone who deals well with his contract, and his income is constantly increasing.

No. 28 — **Expectation:** Patience is a virtue for the rich man; he is always alert, pays attention to what is on the horizon.

No. 29 — **The Prison:** The rich man is solitary; he may be sabotaging himself. The rich man is trapped in a golden cage.

No. 30 — **Legal Matters:** The rich man is interested in counsel and advice, uses his wisdom to restore peace and happiness; the rich man is a lawyer.

No. 31 —   **Short Illness:** The rich man is an insomniac and does not enjoy good health. He may have sexual problems.

No. 32 —   **Grief and Sorrow:** The rich man is a depressive, addicted person.

No. 33 —   **Murky Thoughts:** The younger male always sees the glass half empty, likes to keep himself worrying with dark thoughts.

No. 34 —   **Occupation:** Hardworking, motivated, ambitious, talented young man.

No. 35 —   **A Long Road:** The rich man is patient in his action, waits for the perfect time to act.

No. 36 —   **Hope, Big Water:** The rich man is a gifted one; he may have psychic abilities or some kind of artistic talent.

SAD NEWS

Keywords
Tears, Sorrow, Strife, Annoyance, Unhappiness, Disappointment

"*N*ot a good omen," this card says! It's all about sad and upsetting news coming from different sources: correspondence, phone calls, text message, and the newspaper.

Hopefully its duration is for a short time unless negative cards come around to reinforce its negative orientation. The surrounding cards will also point out the source and the message related to the sad-news card.

Mantra: I now let go and let God.

Influence: Negative

Direction: None

Quick answer: No

Topic card: Sadness

Card No. 14—Sad News with

No. 1 — **Main Male:** Sad and upsetting news for the male querent.

No. 2 — **Main Female:** Sad and upsetting news for the female querent.

No. 3 — **Marriage:** Sad news concerning an alliance, a commitment, a contract.

No. 4 — **A Meeting:** Upsetting news through an encounter during a festivity or celebration.

No. 5 — **The Good Lord:** Upsetting, sad news for the older man.

No. 6 — **The Good Lady:** Upsetting, sad news for the older woman.

No. 7 — **A Pleasant Letter:** Mixed messages, a bill, upsetting letter.

No. 8 — **False Person:** Upsetting news for or from an enemy; a threat letter.

No. 9 — **A Change:** A sad change, an unfortunate change, a change for the worst.

No. 10 — **A Journey:** Car bill, sad and upsetting news about a travel, discomfort travel.

No. 11 — **Lot of Money:** A large bill, an inheritance, upsetting financial news.

No. 12 — **A Rich Girl:** Sad and upsetting news for the younger male.

No. 13 — **A Rich Man:** Sad and upsetting news for the younger female.

No. 15 — **Success in Love:** Sad and upsetting love letter; heartbreaking news.

No. 16 — **His Thoughts:** Mourning, a constant reflection, falling into a depressive state.

No. 17 — **A Gift:** A sorrowful visit, a painful gift, unexpected challenging news.

No. 18 — **Small Child:** A sick child, naivety causes grief, sad news concerning a child or toddler.

No. 19 — **A Funeral:** Mourning, grieving, news of someone passing, news of a funeral.

No. 20 — **The House:** Sad news for the family, worry about the home, sad family member, feeling uncomfortable around the house.

No. 21 — **The Living Room:** Sad news for the close family, feeling uncomfortable around the apartment, sad news is kept secret.

No. 22 — **A Military:** Sad official news, a call for military service, a dominant person brings up grief.

No. 23 — **The Court:** Judicial notification, negative verdict; official correspondence.

No. 24 — **The Thievery:** Burden is over, end of grief, a correspondence is lost.

No. 25 — **High Honours:** False nomination; sad news is acknowledged.

No. 26 — **Big Luck:** The sad situation is handled, grief is now over, a lucky turn of events.

No. 27 —   **Unexpected Money:** Sad news for a middle-aged woman; a raise or payment is rejected.

No. 28 —   **Expectation:** Unfulfilled expectation, sad news for a middle-aged woman.

No. 29 —   **The Prison:** Sad message from a prison or hospital, sad or negative news is kept secret.

No. 30 —   **Legal Matters:** A disappointing legal notification, negative news from the lawyer.

No. 31 —   **Short Illness:** Serious illness, learning that someone is sick, upsetting disease.

No. 32 —   **Grief and Sorrow:** Life crisis, a hopeless situation, things are getting worse.

No. 33 —   **Murky Thoughts:** Negative feedback, news brought out fear and discouragement.

No. 34 —   **Occupation:** Sad news from work, unhealthy working environment, receiving a refusal.

No. 35 —   **A Long Road:** Discomfort, bad news coming from far, sad situation that persists.

No. 36 —   **Hope, Big Water:** Sad news from abroad, a hopeless situation, feeling overwhelmingly sad.

Ignore those that make you fearful and sad, that degrade you back towards disease and death.

—RUMI

NO. 15
SUCCESS IN LOVE

Keywords

Love, Loyalty, Romance, Friendship, Successful, Charming

*L*ove is the answer!

The 15 Success in Love card relates to all kinds of commitment and relationship. These relationships can be of a romantic orientation or more toward a business one.

The surrounding cards will add more details to this bond, but in general it is a positive card to have when it comes to partnerships and especially in a love reading.

Mantra: I am a loving and lovable person.

Influence: Positive

Direction: None

Quick answer: Yes

Topic card: Romance

Card No. 15—Success in Love with

No. 1 —   **Main Male:** Loyal seeker, a love affair with the Main Male.

No. 2 —   **Main Female:** Loyal seeker, a love affair with the Main Female.

No. 3 —   **Marriage:** A marriage of love, loyal couple, successful alliance, a lovely couple.

No. 4 —   **A Meeting:** A romantic encounter, a date, a loving and supportive group, a lovely meeting.

No. 5 —   **The Good Lord:** A charming elderly man, an older lover, a loyal elderly man.

No. 6 —   **The Good Lady:** A charming elderly woman, an older lover, a loyal elderly woman.

No. 7 —   **A Pleasant Letter:** A love letter, a declaration of love, a romantic poem.

No. 8 —   **False Person:** Jealousy, not sincere about his or her feelings, false declaration.

No. 9 —   **A Change:** Positive change, a loving change, relocation of a couple, a successful change.

No. 10 —   **A Journey:** A lovely car, a charming journey, a honeymoon, a romantic escapade.

No. 11 —   **Lot of Money:** Love of money, relationship based upon money, successful transactions.

No. 12 —   **A Rich Girl:** A charming young woman, a younger lover, a loyal young woman.

No. 13 —   **A Rich Man:** A charming young man, a younger lover, a loyal young woman.

No. 14 —   **Sad News:** Melancholy, a sad partner, a disappointed partner.

No. 16 —   **His Thoughts:** Loving thoughts, positive thoughts, thinking of one's love life.

No. 17 —   **A Gift:** Flowers, bouquet, romantic gift, romantic surprise, a gift from the heart.

No. 18 —   **Small Child:** A new love, a pregnancy, a fresh love affair, flirt, naive feelings.

No. 19 —   **A Funeral:** A separation, a breakup, an ending.

No. 20 —   **The House:** Lovely home, solid relationship, safe relationship, strong ties.

No. 21 —   **The Living Room:** Lovely apartment, intimate relationship, strong feelings.

No. 22 —   **A Military:** In love with someone in uniform, a dominant partner, an official relationship.

No. 23 — **The Court:** A civil wedding, a fair decision, with negative cards can announce a divorce, they love the rules.

No. 24 — **The Thievery:** A secret love, losing a lover, infidelity, untrusting.

No. 25 — **High Honours:** Love of school, love of education, successful completion, love at last.

No. 26 — **Big Luck:** Successful relationship, protected relationship, abundance of love.

No. 27 — **Unexpected Money:** Middle-aged lover, unexpected love, unexpected feelings.

No. 28 — **Expectation:** Middle-aged lover, expected partner, expected declaration, expected romance.

No. 29 — **The Prison:** Forbidden love, dangerous relationship, caught in a relationship.

No. 30 — **Legal Matters:** A priest, a pastor, a guru, a love expert, a relationship counselor.

No. 31 — **Short Illness:** Sexual disease, a heartbreak, an unhealthy relationship, a heart disease.

No. 32 — **Grief and Sorrow:** Unfaithful partner, sorrow, tears, heartbreak, addicted to sex.

No. 33 — **Murky Thoughts:** Fear of love, disappointment, fear of being loved and to love.

No. 34 — **Occupation:** Love of work, doing what he/she loves, successful career, loyal to duty.

No. 35 — **A Long Road:** Happy ever after, eternal love, long-distance relationship, forever loyal.

No. 36 — **Hope, Big Water:** A spiritual or religious wedding, sea lover, past-life lover, love gives hope.

A REAL READING WITH
SUCCESS IN LOVE

Rebecca came for a reading; she was in love with Olivier and wanted to know if they would construct something together. I shuffled, she cut the cards, and I asked her to pick three cards randomly. Here's what she got:

12 A Rich Girl + 1 Main Male + 15 Success in Love

This draw brought some doubt on the table; I felt like Olivier may have been involved with another young woman, but I want the cards to be clear on that, so I reshuffled. She cut once again and chose three cards:

13 A Rich Man + 16 His Thoughts + 15 Success in Love

A little bit confused by the cards, I told Rebecca that Olivier was involved with another woman, and their relationship was doing great. I asked her if there was a misunderstanding about all that, as the love and relationship she has is only in her head. Rebecca confirmed that Olivier was married; they had met at a convention, and he acted as a gentleman—very caring, good manners. Rebecca had misinterpreted this as love at first sight.

The cards will always tell the truth, in all circumstances, no matter what; we just need to pay attention and be open to their wisdom.

HIS THOUGHTS

Keywords
Thoughts, Preoccupation, Introspection, Observation, Soul Searching,
Contemplation, Meditation, Plans, Dreams

I can read your mind!

His Thoughts is a card that talks about things not yet materialized, things that are on one's mind. Even if this card pictures a male person and is titled "His" Thoughts, it can be the thoughts of a woman too.

The combination with other cards will reveal the person's current thoughts: negative cards will place the querent in a negative mood, lost in confusion, daydreaming, and falling into depression, and positive cards will uplift the mind, help the querent find ingenious solutions, and bring back peace and serenity.

Mantra: Every decision I make
is the right one for me.

Influence: Neutral

Direction: None

Quick answer: Maybe

Topic card: The mind, one's intention

Card No. 16—His Thoughts with

No. 1 — **Main Male:** The male querent is preoccupied with himself; self-reflection, introspection.

No. 2 — **Main Female:** The female querent is preoccupied with herself; self-reflection, introspection.

No. 3 — **Marriage:** Thinking about an alliance, a commitment; thoughts on a deal, on a contract.

No. 4 — **A Meeting:** Thinking about a group, a meeting, an inventory; planning a meeting.

No. 5 — **The Good Lord:** Thinking about an elderly man, making plans with an elderly man, an old plan.

No. 6 — **The Good Lady:** Thinking about an elderly woman, making plans with an elderly woman, an old plan.

No. 7 — **A Pleasant Letter:** Thinking of a message, plans, drawing, inventory, summary, review.

No. 8 — **False Person:** An illusion, a mirage, a bad idea, confused thoughts, mental manipulation.

No. 9 — **A Change:** Changing thoughts and ideas, changing plans, new conviction, "aha" moment.

No. 10 — **A Journey:** Planning a trip, dreamed of car, preoccupied by a car, a locomotion or journey.

No. 11 — **Lot of Money:** Thoughts of money, financial review, creating a financial plan.

No. 12 — **A Rich Girl:** Thinking of a young woman, preoccupied woman, plans with a young woman.

No. 13 — **A Rich Man:** Thinking of a young man, preoccupied man, plans with a young man.

No. 14 — **Sad News:** Melancholy, preoccupation, stress, sorrow, fear thoughts, depression.

No. 15 — **Success in Love:** Loving thoughts, positive thoughts, thinking of one's love life.

No. 17 — **A Gift:** Thinking of a gift, a promising idea, an inspiration, joyous thoughts; thinking of visiting someone.

No. 18 — **Small Child:** Small thoughts, naive and childish thoughts, new idea, silly thoughts.

No. 19 — **A Funeral:** End of preoccupation, finding a solution, thinking out of the box.

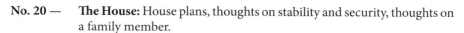

No. 20 — **The House:** House plans, thoughts on stability and security, thoughts on a family member.

No. 21 — **The Living Room:** Intimate thoughts, inner thoughts, thinking of siblings and close family members.

No. 22 — **A Military:** Stubborn and inflexible, keep thoughts in order, self-discipline, strict plans, sticking to a thought or plan.

No. 23 — **The Court:** Official plans, planning a decision, thoughts on legal matters, making a decision.

No. 24 — **The Thievery:** Secret plans, planning a holdup, unfair intention.

No. 25 — **High Honours:** A discovery, an objective, targeted milestone and goals, elevated thoughts.

No. 26 — **Big Luck:** An optimist, a great idea is rewarded, good idea, uplifting thoughts.

No. 27 — **Unexpected Money:** Pondering new resources, indecisive middle-aged woman.

No. 28 — **Expectation:** One's own expectation, one's own plan, an expected idea.

No. 29 — **The Prison:** A blocked plan, planning an outbreak, a stagnation, a standstill.

No. 30 — **Legal Matters:** A legal decision, mental dispute, copyright, pondering advice.

No. 31 — **Short Illness:** Mental illness, schizophrenia, paranoia, lack of focus and concentration.

No. 32 — **Grief and Sorrow:** Mental harassment, depression, thoughts of the past, obsession.

No. 33 — **Murky Thoughts:** Suspicions and doubts, negative thoughts, deception, overestimation.

No. 34 — **Occupation:** Work plans, career plans, work preoccupation, psychologist.

No. 35 — **A Long Road:** Long-term plans, thinking in advance, longtime plan, long-term goals.

No. 36 — **Hope, Big Water:** An intuition, clairsentience, own hopes, spiritually minded.

HIS THOUGHTS CARD
IN A READING

I believe in the power of the mind, that everything we think and speak creates our experience, our tomorrow. Through the years, I've tried successfully to change my thoughts, and for sure I've experienced radical change. In a reading, especially with the Grand Tableau, I look at cards that surround the 16 His Thoughts card. I like to see the mood and the thoughts of my querent, as this will help me understand his situation. I can tell if what is going on is real or simply one's imagination (like with Rebecca's reading).

Often, people believe in things and circumstances that are not real, and take actions accordingly to their thoughts. It's no wonder this person will hit rock bottom. Our mission as a psychic or a card reader is to point out the truth.

*Let go of your mind
and then be mindful.*

—RUMI

NO. 17
A GIFT

Keywords

Present, Visit, Pleasant Surprise, Gratitude,
Exchange, Small Luck

𝒜 wonderful card to have in your reading!

A Gift card announces a visit, that someone is bringing a gift to you both in the literal and figurative sense. Some readers also align this card to children aged less than 12. As always, the surrounding cards will shed more light on the reason and provenance of the gift.

Mantra: I accept all gifts graciously and with deep gratitude.

Influence: Positive

Direction: None

Quick answer: Yes

Topic card: Gifts and offerings

Card No. 17—A Gift with

No. 1 —   **Main Male:** A visit, a gift for the male querent, a happy surprise, a happy time.

No. 2 —   **Main Female:** A visit, a gift for the female querent, a happy surprise, a happy time.

No. 3 —   **Marriage:** Wedding gifts, engagement gift, visited by a couple, happy couple.

No. 4 —   **A Meeting:** Happy group, birthday gift or surprise, a party, a celebration.

No. 5 —   **The Good Lord:** A visit, a gift for the older man, a happy surprise, a happy time.

No. 6 —   **The Good Lady:** A visit, a gift for the older woman, a happy surprise, a happy time.

No. 7 —   **A Pleasant Letter:** A positive message, an invitation, a parcel, a gift coupon, a gift list.

No. 8 —   **False Person:** A wrong gift, an intriguing visit, fake gift (e.g., zirconia instead of a diamond).

No. 9 —   **A Change:** Housewarming gift, surprising change, a happy move, lucky change.

No. 10 —   **A Journey:** A gift of travel, gifting a car, gifting a bicycle or scooter, a happy trip.

No. 11 —   **Lot of Money:** A cash gift, a donation, a gain, lottery prizes, expensive gift.

No. 12 —   **A Rich Girl:** A visit, a gift for the young female, a happy surprise, a happy time.

No. 13 —   **A Rich Man:** A visit, a gift for the young male, a happy surprise, a happy time.

No. 14 —   **Sad News:** A sad visit, a sad surprise, unwanted gift, unpleasant gift.

No. 15 —   **Success in Love:** Gift from the heart, a lovely present, exchange of love, lovely visit.

No. 16 —   **His Thoughts:** Thinking of a gift, thoughtful gift, an inspiration, joyous thoughts, a pleasant visit.

No. 18 —   **Small Child:** Small gift, twins, early visit, gifted child, new gift, cheerful child.

No. 19 —   **A Funeral:** A late visit, an inheritance, a donation, surprising and unexpected end.

No. 20 —   **The House:** Gift of a house, inheriting a house, gifted family, family visit.

No. 21 —   **The Living Room:** Private or secret gift, inheriting an apartment, a family visit.

No. 22 —   **A Military:** Someone in uniform visits; gift of uniform, the right gift, obedient children.

No. 23 —   **The Court:** Adoption, positive decision, positive verdict, welfare fund.

No. 24 —   **The Thievery:** Secret gift, a gift gets lost, risk of kidnapping, a thief visits.

No. 25 —   **High Honours:** Receiving an award; a diplomat; rewarding someone with a gift.

No. 26 —   **Big Luck:** Godsend, a blessing, unexpected help, helpful visit, a positive combo.

No. 27 —   **Unexpected Money:** Unexpected gift, unexpected visitors, a good bargain.

No. 28 —   **Expectation:** Expected gift, middle-aged woman visits, what was expected is finally here.

No. 29 —   **The Prison:** A blocked gift, visiting a prison or hospital, a gift is kept away.

No. 30 —   **Legal Matters:** A positive legal notice, visit of a judicial officer, dealing with inheritance.

No. 31 —   **Short Illness:** A cure, visiting a sick person, childhood disease, sick children.

No. 32 —   **Grief and Sorrow:** Deceiving gift, troublesome visit, a painful gift, painful visit.

No. 33 —   **Murky Thoughts:** Unwanted visit, suspicious gift, fearful visitation, fearful children.

No. 34 —   **Occupation:** A nanny, working with children, flower shop, toy shop, gift shop.

No. 35 —   **A Long Road:** A gift comes from far away, a visitor from afar, a prolonged visit.

No. 36 —   **Hope, Big Water:** Gift of intuition, gifted a voyage or cruise; a gift bring hope to the receiver; an offering.

A REAL READING
WITH THE GIFT

*D*ana and I have been good friends since we were teenagers; she knew about my psychic awareness and my passion for card reading, and I had read for her countless times. The cards had accurately predicted how she would meet a handsome rich man, talented in business, and that he would make her happy.

The cards sometimes have this strange affinity with some people, where they will point out astonishing details that will make your jaw drop, and this was the case for Dana—she was beloved by the cards.

Jamie was on a business trip, and as with many women, Dana was a bit jealous and afraid that her man would meet someone and have an affair. She wanted the cards to reassure her. The cards told her that Jamie loved her and would never betray their love, and next to the male man card was 17 A Gift + **35 A Long Road** + 15 Success in Love. Without any doubt I told her that Jamie will bring her a gift, and it seemed that it was a watch (**long distance**, waiting, time) in the form of a heart (Success in Love). A few days after Jamie arrived, Dana gave me a call, and with excitement she said: "You know what, the cards were right; Jamie gave me a watch in the shape of a heart. It's so beautiful, and I love it."

NO. 18
SMALL CHILD

Keywords

*Curiosity, Naivety, New, Just Starting, Smallness, I
nnocence, Pregnancy, Birth, Morning*

*H*ere we meet the Small Child; it is a card of new beginnings, fresh starts; of smallness, curiosity, and open-mindedness.

It represents a child in your environment, maybe your own. The 18 Small Child does have much knowledge and may often do silly actions. Remember that the cards can be literal and figurative at the same time.

Mantra: I am a perfect child of God.

Influence: Positive

Direction: Facing left

Quick answer: Yes

Topic card: Kids

When the following appear on the LEFT of
No. 18—Small Child

The Future

No. 1 — **Main Male:** The Main Male will experience a new beginning; the querent is naive.

No. 2 — **Main Female:** The Main Female will experience a new beginning; the querent is naive.

No. 3 — **Marriage:** A new marriage, newly born alliance, a new commitment, a fresh agreement.

No. 4 — **A Meeting:** Young couple, newly engaged, newly committed; open-minded couple.

No. 5 — **The Good Lord:** Grandchild—grandfather, a new beginning for the older male, the Good Lord is naive.

No. 6 — **The Good Lady:** Grandchild—grandmother, a new beginning for the older female, the elderly woman is open minded.

No. 7 — **A Pleasant Letter:** A birth certificate, birth announcement, good news, positive correspondence, positive phone calls.

No. 8 — **False Person:** Adopted child, manipulative child, negative start, new enemy, foster parent.

No. 9 — **A Change:** A new phase, early change, starting from scratch, a new direction.

No. 10 — **A Journey:** A positive trip, embarking for a new journey, new car, new ways of locomotion.

No. 11 — **Lot of Money:** New resources, a wealthy child, children's pension, money spent for the kids.

No. 12 — **A Rich Girl:** Talented child, young girl, a daughter, a pregnant young woman, open-minded girl, a carefree person.

No. 13 — **A Rich Man:** Talented child, young boy, a son, a young man caused pregnancy, open-minded guy, a carefree person.

No. 14 — **Sad News:** A sick baby, a crying baby, curiosity leads to problem, a hard situation.

No. 15 — **Success in Love:** Lovely child, lovely baby, new love, open-minded relationship.

No. 16 — **His Thoughts:** New thoughts, new ideas, childish imagination, silly thoughts.

No. 17 — **A Gift:** Gifted child, baby shower, inheritance, early gift, happy visitors.

No. 19 — **A Funeral:** A transition, an abortion, ending and new beginning, life-changing event, opposing energy.

No. 20 — **The House:** Buying a property; family house, childhood home, a kindergarten, a nursery, foster home.

No. 21 — **The Living Room:** A new apartment, a small house, a tiny apartment, a confined room, a tiny personal space.

No. 22 — **A Military:** Setting boundaries, disciplined child, a safe new beginning, authoritative child, child wearing a uniform.

No. 23 — **The Court:** New procedures, adoption procedures, new decision, a silly decision, a silly procedure.

No. 24 — **The Thievery:** Secretive child, unknown child, untrustworthy child, new loss, small loss.

No. 25 — **High Honours:** Known child, recognizing an illegitimate child, a successful child, a rewarded child, a talented child.

No. 26 — **Big Luck:** Lucky beginning, lucky child, a new chance, small luck turn into big one.

No. 27 — **Unexpected Money:** A new contract is in negotiation, unexpected pregnancy, open-minded middle-aged woman.

No. 28 — **Expectation:** New expectation, expecting a pregnancy, a silly expectation, expecting something new.

No. 29 — **The Prison:** Children's hospital, orphanage, a blocked change, a child in difficulty, a lonely child.

No. 30 — **Legal Matters:** Guardianship, new advice, new consultation.

No. 31 — **Short Illness:** A sick child, a delay, a blockage, childhood disease, weak child, sleepy child.

No. 32 — **Grief and Sorrow:** A deceived child, rejected child, abused child, addicted child.

No. 33 — **Murky Thoughts:** A child with negative thoughts, a daydreamer, an upcoming depression, worries caused by a child.

No. 34 — **Occupation:** Working with children, a hard-working child, small job, teacher, caretaker.

No. 35 — **A Long Road:** A new project on its way, showing a lot of patience, a foreign child, baby steps.

No. 36 — **Hope, Big Water:** Spiritual child, a sensitive, small hope.

When the following appear on the RIGHT of
No. 18—Small Child

The Past

No. 1 — **Main Male:** A new beginning has been experienced by the Main Male; the querent was naive.

No. 2 — **Main Female:** A new beginning for the female querent, she was pregnant, the female querent was open minded.

No. 3 — **Marriage:** A past commitment, a past engagement, past agreement.

No. 4 — **A Meeting:** The Small Child was involved in an event such as a baby shower, a christening or a party.

No. 5 — **The Good Lord:** Grandchild—grandfather, a new beginning was experienced by the older male, the good lord was naive.

No. 6 — **The Good Lady:** Grandchild—grandmother, a new beginning was for the older female, the elderly woman was open minded.

No. 7 — **A Pleasant Letter:** Birth certificate, birth announcement, good news, positive correspondence, positive phone calls.

No. 8 — **False Person:** Adopted child, manipulative child, negative start, new enemy, foster parent.

No. 9 — **A Change:** A new phase, early change, starting from scratch, new direction.

No. 10 — **A Journey:** A positive trip, embarking on a new journey, new car, new ways of locomotion.

No. 11 — **Lot of Money:** New resource, a wealthy child, children's pension, money spent for the kids.

No. 12 — **A Rich Girl:** Talented child, young girl, a daughter, a pregnant young woman, open-minded girl, a carefree person.

No. 13 — **A Rich Man:** Talented child, young boy, a son, a young man caused pregnancy, open-minded guy, a carefree person.

No. 14 — **Sad News:** A sick baby, a crying baby, curiosity leads to problem, a hard situation.

No. 15 — **Success in Love:** Lovely child, lovely baby, new love, open-minded relationship.

No. 16 — **His Thoughts:** New thoughts, new ideas, childish imagination, silly thoughts.

No. 17 — **A Gift:** Gifted child, baby shower, inheritance, early gift, happy visitors.

No. 19 — **A Funeral:** A transition, an abortion, ending and new beginning, life-changing event, opposing energies.

No. 20 — **The House:** Buying a property; family house, childhood home, a kindergarten, a nursery, foster home.

No. 21 — **The Living Room:** A new apartment, a small house, a tiny apartment, a confined room, a tiny personal space.

No. 22 — **A Military:** Setting boundaries, disciplined child, a safe new beginning, authoritative child, child wearing a uniform.

No. 23 — **The Court:** New procedures, adoption procedures, new decision, a silly decision, a silly procedure.

No. 24 — **The Thievery:** Secretive child, unknown child, untrustworthy child, new loss, small loss.

No. 25 — **High Honours:** Known child, an illegitimate child was recognized, a successful child, a rewarded child, a talented child.

No. 26 — **Big Luck:** Lucky beginnings, lucky child, a new chance, small luck turns into "big one."

No. 27 — **Unexpected Money:** A new contract was in negotiation, unexpected pregnancy, open-minded middle-aged woman.

No. 28 — **Expectation:** New expectation, expecting a pregnancy, a silly expectation, expecting something new.

No. 29 — **The Prison:** Children's hospital, orphanage, a blocked change, a child in difficulty, a lonely child.

No. 30 — **Legal Matters:** Guardianship, new advice, new consultation.

No. 31 — **Short Illness:** A sick child, delayed, a blockage, childhood disease, weak child, sleepy child.

No. 32 — **Grief and Sorrow:** A deceived child, rejected child, abused child, addicted child.

No. 33 — **Murky Thoughts:** A child with negative thoughts, a daydreamer, an upcoming depression, worries caused by a child.

No. 34 — **Occupation:** Working with children, a hard-working child; small job, teacher, caretaker.

No. 35 — **A Long Road:** A new project on its way, showing a lot of patience, a foreign child, baby steps.

No. 36 — **Hope, Big Water:** Spiritual child, a sensitive, small hope.

When the following appear on the TOP of
No. 18—Small Child

On the Mind

No. 1 — **Main Male:** The child is thinking of his father.

No. 2 — **Main Female:** The child is thinking of his mother.

No. 3 — **Marriage:** The child is thinking of both his parents.

No. 4 — **A Meeting:** The child is thinking of an event; a gathering or party.

No. 5 — **The Good Lord:** The child is thinking of his grandfather or godfather.

No. 6 — **The Good Lady:** The child is thinking of his grandmother or godmother.

No. 7 — **A Pleasant Letter:** The child is thinking of a drawing or a poem.

No. 8 — **False Person:** The child is thinking of a wicked person; he feels someone is an enemy.

No. 9 — **A Change:** The child is thinking of a change, of a new thing happening.

No. 10 — **A Journey:** The child is thinking of a trip, of a bicycle ride, a car ride.

No. 11 — **Lot of Money:** The child is thinking of money.

No. 12 — **A Rich Girl:** The child is thinking of his sister.

No. 13 — **A Rich Man:** The child is thinking of his brother.

No. 14 — **Sad News:** The child is thinking of upsetting news.

No. 15 — **Success in Love:** The child is thinking of the demonstration of love that people shows him.

No. 16 — **His Thoughts:** A daydreamer, imaginative.

No. 17 — **A Gift:** The child is thinking of his gift, of someone visiting.

No. 19 — **A Funeral:** The child is thinking of something ending or someone who had just passed.

No. 20 — **The House:** The child is thinking of his home and family.

No. 21 — **The Living Room:** The child is thinking of his room, of playing space.

No. 22 — **A Military:** The child is thinking of a policeman, fireman, doctor; of a veteran's uniform.

No. 23 — **The Court:** The child is thinking of rights and wrongs, of justice and injustice.

No. 24 — **The Thievery:** The child is thinking of stealing something or someone. He is thinking of a lost item.

No. 25 — **High Honours:** Inventive, talented, gifted child.

No. 26 — **Big Luck:** The child is thinking of a new chance, of being lucky.

No. 27 — **Unexpected Money:** The child is thinking of unexpected gift and money.

No. 28 — **Expectation:** The child is expecting something or someone.

No. 29 — **The Prison:** The child is thinking of his loneliness, of his lack of freedom.

No. 30 — **Legal Matters:** The child is thinking about advice.

No. 31 — **Short Illness:** The child is thinking of his weak health condition and of not being able to sleep properly.

No. 32 — **Grief and Sorrow:** The small child is thinking of difficulties and feels sad.

No. 33 — **Murky Thoughts:** The small child is lost in fear; he thinks of playing a role, a drama.

No. 34 — **Occupation:** The small child is preoccupied; his apprenticeship may be difficult.

No. 35 — **A Long Road:** The child is thinking of a distant destination.

No. 36 — **Hope, Big Water:** The child is fascinated by foreign culture; he may have psychic visions.

When the following appear at the BOTTOM of
No. 18—Small Child

Had Achieved

No. 1 — **Main Male:** The small child has a father.

No. 2 — **Main Female:** The small child has a mother.

No. 3 — **Marriage:** The small child has both parents.

No. 4 — **A Meeting:** The small child is social; he loves being with people.

No. 5 — **The Good Lord:** Is a good and wise child and easy to live with.

No. 6 — **The Good Lady:** Is a good and wise child and easy to live with.

No. 7 — **A Pleasant Letter:** The small child has a pleasant personality, communicates a lot with others, and is often the bearer of joy and happiness.

No. 8 — **False Person:** The small child is playful and manipulates everyone around to get what he wants. An adopted child.

No. 9 — **A Change:** The small child had changed; he is growing up.

No. 10 — **A Journey:** The small child has a love for cars and enjoys the ride.

No. 11 — **Lot of Money:** A wealthy and blessed child.

No. 12 — **A Rich Girl:** He is the small child to his sister or to a young female relative. He is a spoiled child.

No. 13 — **A Rich Man:** The small child is close to his brother or to a young male relative. He is a spoiled child.

No. 14 — **Sad News:** The small child has a displeasing personality; he complains about everything.

No. 15 — **Success in Love:** The small child is lovely and precious.

No. 16 — **His Thoughts:** The young child is a daydreamer.

No. 17 — **A Gift:** The small child loves to give and receive; he has a surprising personality and is known to be a gift to others.

No. 19 — **A Funeral:** The small child is experiencing an ending, a separation, or death.

No. 20 — **The House:** The small child is very close with family.

No. 21 — **The Living Room:** The small child is secretive and likes to be in his own room.

No. 22 — **A Military:** The small child likes discipline and order.

No. 23 — **The Court:** The small child is a wise child.

No. 24 — **The Thievery:** The small child takes things away; he tends to steal from others and snatches what he wants.

No. 25 — **High Honours:** The small child is a gifted child.

No. 26 — **Big Luck:** The small child is a lucky child.

No. 27 — **Unexpected Money:** The child is financially supported, a surprising child, unexpected gift.

No. 28 — **Expectation:** The small child is patient.

No. 29 — **The Prison:** A solitary child.

No. 30 — **Legal Matters:** An adopted child.

No. 31 — **Short Illness:** A sick child, childhood illness.

No. 32 — **Grief and Sorrow:** A depressive child, an addicted child.

No. 33 — **Murky Thoughts:** The small child is a negative, pessimistic young child.

No. 34 — **Occupation:** Hardworking, motivated child.

No. 35 — **A Long Road:** A patient child, adopted child.

No. 36 — **Hope, Big Water:** A gifted child; he may have psychic abilities; a born artist.

NO. 19
A FUNERAL

Keywords

*Ending, Transformation, Death, Evening, Darkness, Termination,
Painfulness, Definitive, Irreversible, Conclusion*

*L*ike the Death card in Tarot, many people fear 19 A Funeral card as it is related to death. Worry not! When this card appears in your reading, it is not telling you that you are going to die in the forthcoming days. It's an indication that something had ended, that you are in a transformative state; like the butterfly, you are metamorphosing.

Some readers will look at the card the coffin is pointing to, as this card will indicate in what area the transformation and ending is occurring. With negative cards, of course these changes can be hard and difficult. The surrounding cards will shed light on the influence of the funeral in your reading.

Mantra: I am ready to make changes in my life.

Influence: Negative

Direction: None

Quick answer: No

Topic card: Endings and transitions

143

Card No. 19—A Funeral with

No. 1 — **Main Male:** A change, a transformative situation for the Main Male, an ending or a separation.

No. 2 — **Main Female:** A change, a transformative situation for the Main Female, an ending or a separation.

No. 3 — **Marriage:** A divorce, a definitive separation, ending of marital life, unhappy marriage, a dead relationship.

No. 4 — **A Meeting:** A funeral procession, a fruitless negotiation, a nightly meeting, a transformative group.

No. 5 — **The Good Lord:** A change, a transformative situation for the older male, an ending or a separation.

No. 6 — **The Good Lady:** A change, a transformative situation for the older female, an ending or a separation.

No. 7 — **A Pleasant Letter:** A death certificate, a message of someone's passing, a negative letter, news that brought a new beginning.

No. 8 — **False Person:** An unfair ending, a wrong separation, painful manipulative person, using grief as excuse, end of secrets.

No. 9 — **A Change:** A big transformation, saying goodbye, definitive situation, irreversible change, a blocked change.

No. 10 — **A Journey:** Going to a funeral, evening travel, a journey of no return, a road accident, a last journey.

No. 11 — **Lot of Money:** Inheritance, legacy, funeral expenditure, ruin, end of lease, money kept or buried.

No. 12 — **A Rich Girl:** A change, a transformative situation for the younger female, an ending or a separation.

No. 13 — **A Rich Man:** A change, a transformative situation for the younger male, an ending or a separation.

No. 14 — **Sad News:** Message of someone's passing, a sad ending, end of a chapter, a sad conclusion.

No. 15 — **Success in Love:** End of love, a separation, a heartbreak, a breakup, saying goodbye to a loved one.

No. 16 — **His Thoughts:** Worrying about death, a mental conclusion, worrying about a separation, dark thoughts.

No. 17 — **A Gift:** An inheritance, a donation, an evening visit, an ultimate gift, a last visit, a spirit visitation.

No. 18 — **Small Child:** A transition, an abortion, ending and then a new beginning, life-changing event, opposing energies.

No. 20 — **The House:** Leaving the house, leaving the family, selling a house, definitive residence, the last home.

No. 21 — **The Living Room:** A tomb or grave, moving from an apartment, end of secrets, end of privacy.

No. 22 — **A Military:** Official funeral, end of military service, right conclusion, official notification of death.

No. 23 — **The Court:** End of administrative procedure, a definite verdict, an inheritance, a donation.

No. 24 — **The Thievery:** Keeping a death secret, burying stolen things, identity usurpation, definitive loss.

No. 25 — **High Honours:** A glorious funeral, a rejected award, a blocked reward, glory and fame after death.

No. 26 — **Big Luck:** A blessed change, a positive termination, an amazing transformation, a blessed funeral.

No. 27 — **Unexpected Money:** Sudden and unexpected passing, an inheritance, a donation, a middle-aged female passed.

No. 28 — **Expectation:** Expected death, expected ending, awaited separation, expecting finality.

No. 29 — **The Prison:** Set free, end of hospitalization, dying in the hospital, a blocked change.

No. 30 — **Legal Matters:** Inheritance or donation, end of hostility, end of a therapy, a verdict, a definitive decision.

No. 31 — **Short Illness:** Depending on the question, it can be aggravated illness or end of illness.

No. 32 — **Grief and Sorrow:** Despairing situation, unable to recover from grief, a great deception, painful situation.

No. 33 — **Murky Thoughts:** Anxiety, depression, grief is overwhelming, negative thoughts, painful thoughts.

No. 34 — **Occupation:** Retirement, career reconversion, getting fired, end of a job contract, working for a funeral home.

No. 35 — **A Long Road:** Slow death, a slow change, slow motion, a fateful change.

No. 36 — **Hope, Big Water:** Mediumship, loved ones in heaven, end of hope, a spiritual death, near-death experience.

A REAL READING WITH
A FUNERAL CARD

A Funeral card is so misunderstood by people because the motion picture industry created a fear in their horror movies when the first card of the Tarot, flying out of the deck and onto the table, would be Death—and this freaked everybody out. But in a real-life reading, the Death card from the Tarot or 18 The Funeral card from the Kipper doesn't announce death; it's simply a shift, a no-going-back-from once the transition has taken place.

Vanessa has worked for a big company for a long time now; she was expecting a promotion and wanted to have more details regarding whether she would finally get one. For a yes or no reading, I usually pull only two cards, as too many cards will confuse the answer; then I can add a clarifying card if needed. The cards that came out for her were

34 Occupation + 19 A Funeral

We see here that there is an ending in work, a transition, leaving a position or a start to a new one—and this shift is irreversible. I felt that the answer was incomplete, so I asked Vanessa to pull another card to clarify the reading. She pulled the 25 High Honours. The answer is crystal clear; Vanessa would get her promotion and be acknowledged for her hard work. See, no one had died here!

THE HOUSE

Keywords

*Home, Property, Family, Family Life, Foundation,
Ownership, Security, Safety, Stability*

*S*tanding strong and tall, the House represents your home, your family, the people you care about, the place you feel safe, or your place of residence. When the House comes in a reading, it will speak of different things that will depend on your question; sometimes it will be property or ownership, and other times it will be security, safety, and stability.

No need to be afraid when you see the House card next to you, giving you strength and courage to deal with life.

Mantra: I am at home; I am safe.

Influence: Positive

Direction: None

Quick answer: Yes

Topic card: Home, family, property

Card No. 20—The House with

No. 1 — **Main Male:** The male querent's house, family, and property. A cozy man, a safe partner.

No. 2 — **Main Female:** The female querent's house, family, and property. A cozy woman, a safe partner.

No. 3 — **Marriage:** Harmonious family life, a safe couple, a solid couple, a safe relationship.

No. 4 — **A Meeting:** A meeting will be held in a house; housewarming, a closed society, a network of relationships, the family.

No. 5 — **The Good Lord:** An elder man from a good family, a protector, male spirit guide or ancestor, a father, a grandfather, an uncle.

No. 6 — **The Good Lady:** An elderly woman from a good family, a protector, female spirit guide or ancestor, mother, a grandmother, an aunt.

No. 7 — **A Pleasant Letter:** Family correspondence, property contract, a safe letter, news from family.

No. 8 — **False Person:** Wrong house, manipulative family member, bad neighborhood, family jealousy.

No. 9 — **A Change:** House renovation, moving house, a change in the family, new family member.

No. 10 — **A Journey:** Safe travel, visiting family, family car, family trip, a secondary residence.

No. 11 — **Lot of Money:** Inheritance, legacy, buying a house, house expenditure, family fortune.

No. 12 — **A Rich Girl:** A young girl from a good family, a protector, young female spirit guide or ancestor, a sister, a daughter, a niece.

No. 13 — **A Rich Man:** A young man from a good family, a protector, young male spirit guide or ancestor, a brother, a son, a nephew.

No. 14 — **Sad News:** Family worries, sadness in the family, family problems, family's sad history.

No. 15 — **Success in Love:** Lovely home, peaceful family, strong bond, love from the family, a loving family.

No. 16 — **His Thoughts:** Family worries, house plans, security plans, thinking of a property.

No. 17 — **A Gift:** Inheritance, a donation, a gift for the house, a visitor coming along, a safe gift.

No. 18 — **Small Child:** A new house, a small house, a nursery, a foster home, a safe place for children.

No. 19 — **A Funeral:** Leaving the house, leaving the family, selling a house, definitive residence, last home.

No. 21 — **The Living Room:** A private room, home office, solid foundation, secret room.

No. 22 — **A Military:** Police station, fire brigade, authoritative family member, a safe place, right house, under an alarm system.

No. 23 — **The Court:** Land registration, real-estate administrative procedures, property right, legal affair involving property.

No. 24 — **The Thievery:** Losing a house, family secret, burglars, unsafe house, a thief among the family.

No. 25 — **High Honours:** A university, a prestigious house, a fraternity, a sorority, a respectful and prestigious family.

No. 26 — **Big Luck:** A casino, a gambling house, a successful family, lucky family, fortunate home.

No. 27 — **Unexpected Money:** Unexpected bills, middle-aged neighbor, bank, saving account.

No. 28 — **Expectation:** Presumption between family member, expectation on a house, family anticipation.

No. 29 — **The Prison:** A sanatorium, in a rest house, hospice, care center, housebound.

No. 30 — **Legal Matters:** Consult a housing expert, a real-estate agency, family therapy.

No. 31 — **Short Illness:** Home hospitalization, sick family member, stress in family, a hereditary disease.

No. 32 — **Grief and Sorrow:** Family deception, addicted family, family conflict, shaky foundation, unsolved family problem.

No. 33 — **Murky Thoughts:** Anxious, depressive family. Family with secrets, not sharing their thoughts; a frightened family.

No. 34 — **Occupation:** Home office, working from home, family company, freelance worker, safe work, working with family.

No. 35 — **A Long Road:** A secondary residence far away, family members living far away, acquiring a house will take time.

No. 36 — **Hope, Big Water:** Spiritual house, spiritual family, house near the waters, a foreign secondary residence.

Card No. 20—The House

as the center card, tells us that "The new house is a sanctuary of love."

NO. 21
THE LIVING ROOM

Keywords
Apartment, Privacy, Kitchen, Craft Room, Personal Space, Confined Environment, Comfort

The Living Room is the second card that relates to family ties and property. Contrarily to The House, the space is restricted, things are more intimate; it's the heart of the house where private things happen.

The Living Room often appears in my readings as a personal, sacred space, where the querent gathers his thoughts and creates plans. In terms of housing, 21 The Living Room is more of an apartment type, a small private residence.

> **Mantra:** I bless my space with love,
> and I place love in each corner.
>
> **Influence:** Positive
>
> **Direction:** None
>
> **Quick answer:** Yes
>
> **Topic card:** Intimacy and privacy

Card No. 21—The Living Room with

No. 1 —   **Main Male:** Intimacy and privacy of the male querent, the male querent feels at home, the male querent is discreet.

No. 2 —   **Main Female:** Intimacy and privacy of the female querent, the female querent feels at home, the female querent is discreet.

No. 3 —   **Marriage:** Couple intimacy, couple's private life, feeling at ease together.

No. 4 —   **A Meeting:** A private meeting, secret ceremony, tight circle of friends, private gathering.

No. 5 —   **The Good Lord:** Intimacy and privacy of the older male, the older male feels at home, the older male is discreet.

No. 6 —   **The Good Lady:** Intimacy and privacy of the older female, the older female feels at home, the elder female is discreet.

No. 7 —   **A Pleasant Letter:** A private letter, intimate conversation, property contract, secret letter.

No. 8 —   **False Person:** Envy and traitors are close to you; pay attention to your surroundings, a wrong environment.

No. 9 —   **A Change:** An intimate change, moving house or apartment, renovation and redecoration, a change in the family.

No. 10 —   **A Journey:** Secret travel, a personal trip, visiting a family member, a private car.

No. 11 —   **Lot of Money:** Money for the family, an inheritance; purchasing an apartment, a condominium; loan and mortgage.

No. 12 —   **A Rich Girl:** Intimacy and privacy for the younger female, the younger female feels at home, the younger female is discreet.

No. 13 —   **A Rich Man:** Intimacy and privacy for the younger male, the younger male feels at home, the younger male is discreet.

No. 14 —   **Sad News:** Sad news for the close family, feeling uncomfortable around the apartment, sad news is kept secret.

No. 15 —   **Success in Love:** Lovely apartment, intimate relationship, strong feelings.

No. 16 —   **His Thoughts:** Intimate thoughts, inner thoughts, thinking of siblings and close family members.

No. 17 —   **A Gift:** Private or secret gift, inheriting an apartment, family visit.

No. 18 —   **Small Child:** A new apartment, a small house, a tiny apartment, a confined room, a tiny personal space.

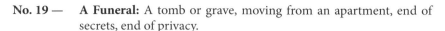

No. 19 — **A Funeral:** A tomb or grave, moving from an apartment, end of secrets, end of privacy.

No. 20 — **The House:** Leaving the house, leaving the family, selling a house, definitive residence, last home.

No. 22 — **A Military:** A safe haven, a protected apartment, under an alarm system, the right apartment.

No. 23 — **The Court:** Land registration, real-estate administrative procedures, property right, legal affairs involving ownership.

No. 24 — **The Thievery:** Loss of intimacy; burglars, unsafe apartment, a thief among the family.

No. 25 — **High Honours:** Private lessons, private tuition, a laureate.

No. 26 — **Big Luck:** A successful family, lucky family, valuable intimacy, personal happiness, one's own luck.

No. 27 — **Unexpected Money:** Unexpected bills, middle-aged neighbor, purchasing an apartment.

No. 28 — **Expectation:** Presumption between family members, expectation on a house, family anticipation.

No. 29 — **The Prison:** A building, a block of apartments, arrest room, specialized hospital.

No. 30 — **Legal Matters:** Consulting a housing expert, a real-estate agency, family therapy.

No. 31 — **Short Illness:** Sick family member, private life is affected, an infirmary, forced to rest.

No. 32 — **Grief and Sorrow:** Unsolved personal problems, private life is in decadence, deceived by private life.

No. 33 — **Murky Thoughts:** Anxious about one's private life, is worried about an apartment, has private secrets.

No. 34 — **Occupation:** Home office, working from home, freelance worker, housekeeping, working with family.

No. 35 — **A Long Road:** A secondary residence far away, family members living far away, acquiring an apartment will take time.

No. 36 — **Hope, Big Water:** Sacred space, an apartment by the waters, there is hope on an apartment.

Both The House and The Living Room cards talk about your place of residence. The Living Room is more of a private area, related to private life. Not everyone has access to 21 The Living Room; precious and beautiful items are displayed, and private and intimate conversation takes place there.

The house is more of a large circle people can access—other areas may be more private. We can share our house but not our private space.

A MILITARY

Keywords
Someone in Uniform, Public Authority, Domination, Rightness, Discipline, and Order

A Military represents discipline, rightness, and domination. He is seen as a negative omen in the Kipper; this is due to the fear people had of the Bavarian militia.

A Military incarnates people who wear a uniform—for instance, a police officer, fireman, doctor, nurse, et al. In a situation, this card would ask for structure and order; it's a card that certifies an event, a feeling, a doubt, or an insight. Surrounding cards will add more details and precision.

Mantra: I am the ruler of my own life.

Influence: Negative

Direction: Facing left

Quick answer: No

Topic card: Person in uniform

When the following appear on the LEFT of
No. 22—A Military

The Future

No. 1 — **Main Male:** The person in uniform will interact with the male seeker.

No. 2 — **Main Female:** The person in uniform will interact with the female seeker.

No. 3 — **Marriage:** The person in uniform will interact with a couple.

No. 4 — **A Meeting:** The person in uniform will interact with a group of people or will be assisting at a meeting.

No. 5 — **The Good Lord:** The person in uniform will interact with the elderly man.

No. 6 — **The Good Lady:** The person in uniform will interact with the elderly woman.

No. 7 — **A Pleasant Letter:** Good news, news to come, positive correspondence, positive phone calls for the person in uniform.

No. 8 — **False Person:** The person in uniform interacts with a rival; cunning, dangerous person, fraudulent officer!

No. 9 — **A Change:** A change is imminent, the military will move or relocate, a planned change will succeed.

No. 10 — **A Journey:** Planned changes will succeed, a positive trip, the military embarks on a journey.

No. 11 — **Lot of Money:** Financial stability, money comes in, wealth and abundance for the person in uniform.

No. 12 — **A Rich Girl:** Interaction with a daughter, a sister, or any young female relative; closeness with a young female, a young lover for the person in uniform.

No. 13 — **A Rich Man:** Interaction with a son, a brother, or any young male relative; closeness with a young male, a young lover for the person in uniform.

No. 14 — **Sad News:** The person in uniform receives negative or sad news; a depressed mood, dealing with some bad news.

No. 15 — **Success in Love:** The person in uniform falls in love; love affair, a happy and positive love life.

No. 16 — **His Thoughts:** The person in uniform is preoccupied, very thoughtful; lots going on in his mind.

No. 17 — **A Gift:** External circumstances bring joy to the person in uniform; a gift, a pleasant visit.

No. 18 — **Small Child:** A new beginning, a pregnancy, a disciplined child, the person in uniform interacts with a child.

No. 19 — **A Funeral:** An ending, a separation for the person in uniform, assisting with an official funeral, military funeral honors.

No. 20 — **The House:** The person in uniform's house, family member, or headquarters.

No. 21 — **The Living Room:** The person in uniform feels at home, his personal space, guarded and protected environment.

No. 23 — **The Court:** Police officer, someone under oath, a final verdict, justice triumphs, official matter will be regulated.

No. 24 — **The Thievery:** Corrupted officer, the police arrest the thief, the stolen item is recovered by the police.

No. 25 — **High Honours:** Military award, military career, civil service.

No. 26 — **Big Luck:** Self-discipline is paying off; the person in uniform is happy.

No. 27 — **Unexpected Money:** A windfall, unexpected happy surprise for the person in uniform, interacting with a middle-aged woman.

No. 28 — **Expectation:** The person in uniform is patient and has strong desires; the next card will say what kind of expectation he has.

No. 29 — **The Prison:** Hospital worker, prison guard, policeman.

No. 30 — **Legal Matters:** Seeing a lawyer, seeking expertise, dealing with legal matters.

No. 31 — **Short Illness:** A doctor, a therapist, medical advice, self-discipline is required to heal.

No. 32 — **Grief and Sorrow:** A difficult time to come, problems and difficulties pile up before the person in uniform, a pattern, a depression, an addiction.

No. 33 — **Murky Thoughts:** Negative mood, afraid of the police, hiding something from the police.

No. 34 — **Occupation:** Policeman, doctor, fireman, nurse, hierarchy, a profession that requires self-discipline.

No. 35 — **A Long Road:** The person in uniform travels to a distant destination; patience—things will not happen now.

No. 36 — **Hope, Big Water:** Traveling abroad, crossing waters, event will happen in a foreign land, feeling hopeful.

When the following appear on the RIGHT of
No. 22—A Military
———•·•———

The Past

No. 1 — **Main Male:** The person in uniform has interacted with the male seeker.

No. 2 — **Main Female:** The person in uniform has interacted with the female seeker.

No. 3 — **Marriage:** The person in uniform has interacted with a couple.

No. 4 — **A Meeting:** The person in uniform has interacted with a group of people or will be assisting at a meeting.

No. 5 — **The Good Lord:** The person in uniform has interacted with the elderly man.

No. 6 — **The Good Lady:** The person in uniform has interacted with the elderly woman.

No. 7 — **A Pleasant Letter:** The person in uniform has received positive news, correspondence, or a phone call.

No. 8 — **False Person:** The person in uniform had interacted with a rival, with a cunning, dangerous person.

No. 9 — **A Change:** A change has occurred, A Military had moved or relocated, a change in his plan has succeeded.

No. 10 — **A Journey:** A change in his plan has succeeded, a positive trip, A Military has embarked on a journey.

No. 11 — **Lot of Money:** Financial stability, money comes, wealth and abundance for the person in uniform.

No. 12 — **A Rich Girl:** Interacted with a daughter, a sister, or any young female relative; closeness with a young female, a former young lover.

No. 13 — **A Rich Man:** Interacted with a son, a brother, or any young male relative; closeness with a young male, a former young lover.

No. 14 — **Sad News:** The person in uniform received negative or sad news; a depressed mood, dealt with some bad news.

No. 15 — **Success in Love:** The person in uniform was in love or was involved in a love affair, was in a happy and positive love life.

No. 16 — **His Thoughts:** The person in uniform was preoccupied, thoughtful; lots was going on in his mind.

No. 17 — **A Gift:** External circumstances have brought joy to the person in uniform; a gift, a pleasant visit.

No. 18 — **Small Child:** The person in uniform has been through a new beginning, a pregnancy. A disciplined child.

No. 19 — **A Funeral:** The person in uniform experienced an ending, a separation; he assisted at an official funeral, a military funeral honors.

No. 20 — **The House:** The person in uniform's house, roots, family member, or headquarters.

No. 21 — **The Living Room:** The person in uniform felt at home, his personal space, guarded and protected environment.

No. 23 — **The Court:** Police officer, someone under oath, a final verdict, justice triumphs, official matter was regulated.

No. 24 — **The Thievery:** Corrupted officer, the police arrested the thief, the stolen items were recovered by the police, or the thief escaped.

No. 25 — **High Honours:** Military award, military career, civil service.

No. 26 — **Big Luck:** Self-discipline has paid off; the person in uniform was happy.

No. 27 — **Unexpected Money:** A windfall, unexpected happy surprise for the person in uniform, a middle-aged woman from the past.

No. 28 — **Expectation:** The person in uniform was patient and had strong desires; the next card will say what kind of expectation he had.

No. 29 — **The Prison:** Hospital worker, prison guard, policeman.

No. 30 — **Legal Matters:** The man in uniform was seeing a lawyer, seeking expertise, dealt with legal matters.

No. 31 — **Short Illness:** A doctor, a therapist, medical advice, self-discipline was required to heal.

No. 32 — **Grief and Sorrow:** Been through a difficult time, problems and difficulties were piling up before the person in uniform, a pattern, a depression, an addiction.

No. 33 — **Murky Thoughts:** Negative mood, fear of the police, hiding something from the police.

No. 34 — **Occupation:** Policeman, doctor, fireman, nurse, hierarchy, a profession that requires self-discipline.

No. 35 — **A Long Road:** The person in uniform traveled to a distant destination; he has shown a lot of patience.

No. 36 — **Hope, Big Water:** Traveling abroad, crossing waters, event that had happened in a foreign land, the man in uniform felt hopeful.

When the following appear on the TOP of
No. 22—A Military

On the Mind

No. 1 — **Main Male:** The person in uniform is thinking of a particular man: his partner, a significant man in his life.

No. 2 — **Main Female:** The person in uniform is thinking of a particular woman: his spouse, his partner, a significant woman in his life.

No. 3 — **Marriage:** The person in uniform dreams of a harmonious relationship; thinking about a future partnership or deal.

No. 4 — **A Meeting:** The person in uniform is thinking of an appointment, a social gathering, an event, meeting a group.

No. 5 — **The Good Lord:** The person in uniform is thinking of an older man, a supportive friend, a father.

No. 6 — **The Good Lady:** The person in uniform is thinking of an older woman, supportive female friend.

No. 7 — **A Pleasant Letter:** The person in uniform longs for better communication; thinking of a message or a correspondence.

No. 8 — **False Person:** The person in uniform is thinking of an enemy, a rival, a cunning, dangerous person.

No. 9 — **A Change:** The person in uniform is thinking of a change, of a move or a relocation; thinking of a change.

No. 10 — **A Journey:** The person in uniform is thinking of a planned change, of a trip. Longing for a particular destination.

No. 11 — **Lot of Money:** The person in uniform is thinking of his financial stability, constantly thinking of his finances; money is very important for him.

No. 12 — **A Rich Girl:** The person in uniform is thinking of a daughter, a sister, or any young female relative; thinking of a young lover.

No. 13 — **A Rich Man:** The person in uniform is thinking of a son, a brother, or any young male relative; thinking of a young lover.

No. 14 — **Sad News:** The person has sorrowful thoughts, a fear of bad news. Negative thoughts.

No. 15 — **Success in Love:** The person in uniform is thinking of success, thinking of his love life.

No. 16 — **His Thoughts:** The person in uniform is thinking a lot right now; lots is going on his mind.

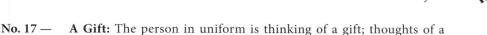

No. 17 — **A Gift:** The person in uniform is thinking of a gift; thoughts of a pleasant visit.

No. 18 — **Small Child:** The person in uniform is thinking of a new beginning, innocent thoughts, naive thoughts, planning something new, thinking of a baby.

No. 19 — **A Funeral:** The person in uniform is thinking of an ending, of a separation, thinking of a funeral.

No. 20 — **The House:** The person in uniform is thinking of a property, of constructing something.

No. 21 — **The Living Room:** The person in uniform is thinking of his private life, thinking of things going on around the house.

No. 23 — **The Court:** The person in uniform is thinking of a legal issue, thinking about an important decision, thinking of a deadline.

No. 24 — **The Thievery:** The person in uniform is thinking of a lost object, reviewing a loss; the person in uniform thinks of taking something away.

No. 25 — **High Honours:** The person in uniform thinks about studying; he is intelligent and aware of his talents and capacity.

No. 26 — **Big Luck:** The person in uniform acknowledges his luck, of the various doors opening before him.

No. 27 — **Unexpected Money:** The person in uniform thinks of a contract, of a lucrative deal; he may also be worried by his finances at the moment.

No. 28 — **Expectation:** The person in uniform is thinking of a middle-aged woman, thinking about his goals and motives, thinking about the future of things.

No. 29 — **The Prison:** The person in uniform is thinking about his loneliness, dreaming of freedom.

No. 30 — **Legal Matters:** The person in uniform is considering the help of a lawyer, considering legal disputes.

No. 31 — **Short Illness:** The person in uniform is thinking about his weak health condition, he is an insomniac, he should uplift his thought in this situation.

No. 32 — **Grief and Sorrow:** The person in uniform is thinking of a difficult time to come, problems and difficulties are piling up, facing a depression, even an addiction.

No. 33 — **Murky Thoughts:** Negative mood; the person in uniform is lost in fear; drama queen, negative thinking.

No. 34 — **Occupation:** Preoccupied by his work, the person in uniform's work involved a lot of his logic and intelligence.

No. 35 — **A Long Road:** Thinking of a distant destination, the person in uniform plans things in advance.

No. 36 — **Hope, Big Water:** The person in uniform is fascinated by foreign culture, needs to ground himself.

When the following appear at the BOTTOM of
No. 22—A Military

Has Achieved

No. 1 — **Main Male:** The person in uniform has a partner, someone significant in his life.

No. 2 — **Main Female:** The person in uniform has a spouse, has someone significant in his [[**her?**]] life.

No. 3 — **Marriage:** The person in uniform is a happily married man; he is in a committed relationship/partnership, achieved positive deals and contracts.

No. 4 — **A Meeting:** The person in uniform is a very social person, involved in many events, gatherings, and get-togethers.

No. 5 — **The Good Lord:** The person in uniform is a good person, supportive of his friends, and a good father.

No. 6 — **The Good Lady:** The person in uniform is a good person, supportive of her friends.

No. 7 — **A Pleasant Letter:** The person in uniform has a pleasant personality, communicates a lot with others, and is often the bearer of good news.

No. 8 — **False Person:** The person in uniform may be sabotaging himself; he is his own rival. He has a cunning personality and needs to change the way he behaves in life.

No. 9 — **A Change:** The person in uniform is a changed man; he had been through the whole process, even relocating.

No. 10 — **A Journey:** The person in uniform travels a lot, his work may involve travel, he may control the traffic.

No. 11 — **Lot of Money:** The person in uniform has achieved financial stability; he is in control of his budget.

No. 12 — **A Rich Girl:** The person in uniform is close to his daughter, sister, or any young female relative; she acts as a spoiled child.

No. 13 — **A Rich Man:** The person in uniform is close to his son, brother, or any young male relative; he acts as a spoiled child.

No. 14 — **Sad News:** The person in uniform has a displeasing personality, complains about everything, and is often the bearer of bad news.

No. 15 — **Success in Love:** The person in uniform is a loyal partner, tied to his intention, respectful of his relationship, can be trusted 100%.

No. 16 — **His Thoughts:** The person in uniform is more of an action man than someone who planned things in advance; he is more logical than practical.

No. 17 — **A Gift:** The person in uniform loves to give and receive, has a surprising personality, and is known to be a gift to others.

No. 18 — **Small Child:** The person in uniform had achieved new beginning, is a father to come, can also be someone with a naive personality.

No. 19 — **A Funeral:** The person in uniform had closely experienced an ending, a separation, or death.

No. 20 — **The House:** The person in uniform is the owner of his property; a cozy man, he is a family man, tied to family values.

No. 21 — **The Living Room:** The person in uniform is a secretive man, protecting his privacy and intimacy; very attached to his home.

No. 23 — **The Court:** High minded, the person in uniform is someone who has principles; he always honors deadlines.

No. 24 — **The Thievery:** The person in uniform is corrupt; he tends to steal from other people and snatches what he wants.

No. 25 — **High Honours:** The person in uniform is acknowledged, enjoys a good reputation, and is seen as a leader.

No. 26 — **Big Luck:** The person in uniform is a lucky man; he acknowledges it and uses his luck in every one of his ventures.

No. 27 — **Unexpected Money:** The person in uniform is someone who deals well with his contract, and his income is constantly increasing.

No. 28 — **Expectation:** Patience is a virtue for the person in uniform; he is always alert, paying attention to what is on the horizon.

No. 29 — **The Prison:** The person in uniform is solitary; he may be sabotaging himself.

No. 30 — **Legal Matters:** The person in uniform is interested in counsel and advice and uses his wisdom to restore peace and happiness.

No. 31 — **Short Illness:** The person in uniform is an insomniac and does not enjoy good health. He may have sexual problems.

No. 32 — **Grief and Sorrow:** The person in uniform is depressive, is an addicted person.

No. 33 — **Murky Thoughts:** Always sees the glass half empty, likes to keep himself worrying with dark thoughts.

No. 34 — **Occupation:** Hardworking, motivated, disciplined, ambitious man.

No. 35 — **A Long Road:** The person in uniform is patient in his actions and waits for the perfect time to act.

No. 36 — **Hope, Big Water:** The person in uniform is a gifted one; he may have psychic abilities or any kind of artistic talent.

Seek self-discipline with all your soul.

—RUMI

THE COURT

Keywords

Administrative Procedures, Legal Decision,
Legal Dispute, Lawsuit, Justice, Verdict

*T*he Court card is seen under a negative umbrella, like with 22 A Military; in the time of the Kipper's creation, people were quite afraid of being involved with justice, as they believed that law was unfair and against them.

I tend to see this card under a neutral orientation; in my readings, it talks about legal or administrative procedures, a public building that has to do with law and order. Combination with other cards brings more clarity to what 23 The Court can mean.

> **Mantra:** My choices are always right.
>
> **Influence:** Neutral to negative
>
> **Direction:** None
>
> **Quick answer:** No—maybe
>
> **Topic card:** Endings and transition

Card No. 23—The Court with

No. 1 — **Main Male:** The male querent is dealing with legal matters, is in the middle of an administrative procedure, waits for a decision.

No. 2 — **Main Female:** The female querent is dealing with legal matters, is in the middle of an administrative procedure, waits for a decision.

No. 3 — **Marriage:** A divorced, definitive separation; ending of marital life; unhappy marriage; a dead relationship.

No. 4 — **A Meeting:** A court date, witness in a trial, a negotiation, an important decision.

No. 5 — **The Good Lord:** The elder male is dealing with legal matters, is in the middle of an administrative procedure, waits for a decision.

No. 6 — **The Good Lady:** The elder female is dealing with legal matters, is in the middle of an administrative procedure, waits for a decision.

No. 7 — **A Pleasant Letter:** A positive decision, a positive verdict, important document, a legal notification.

No. 8 — **False Person:** An unfair verdict, a wrong decision, painful manipulative person, cheat and lies.

No. 9 — **A Change:** A postponed court date, a serious change, a decision is changed.

No. 10 — **A Journey:** Going to the court; applying for a visa, green card, car document; contravention.

No. 11 — **Lot of Money:** Inheritance, legacy, legal expenditures, tax office, bank.

No. 12 — **A Rich Girl:** The younger female is dealing with legal matters, is in the middle of an administrative procedure, waits for a decision.

No. 13 — **A Rich Man:** The younger male is dealing with legal matters, is in the middle of an administrative procedure, waits for a decision.

No. 14 — **Sad News:** Negative verdict, wrong decision, a decision bring sadness and tears.

No. 15 — **Success in Love:** Success procedures, a positive verdict, making a relationship official.

No. 16 — **His Thoughts:** Worrying about justice issues, pondering a decision, in the phase of decision making.

No. 17 — **A Gift:** Inheritance, a donation, surprising decision, a visitor with legal news.

No. 18 — **Small Child:** A new decision, new verdict, family court, guardianship, child custody.

No. 19 — **A Funeral:** Inheritance, a donation, end of trial, termination of a legal affair.

No. 20 — **The House:** Property rights, land registry, verdict concerning a property.

No. 21 — **The Living Room:** Property rights, divorce, verdict concerning an apartment.

No. 22 — **A Military:** Police officer, someone under oath, a final verdict, justice triumphs, official matter will be regulated.

No. 24 — **The Thievery:** A secret verdict, a fraud, corrupt court, thief in the hands of justice.

No. 25 — **High Honours:** Civil service, law school, winning a court case.

No. 26 — **Big Luck:** A fair decision, a blessed verdict, happy outcome, a happy end.

No. 27 — **Unexpected Money:** The verdict implies payment, paying for administrative procedures, receiving a compensation.

No. 28 — **Expectation:** An expected decision, an expected verdict, awaited justice, expected judgment.

No. 29 — **The Prison:** The lawsuit leads to imprisonment, a government decree, an official verdict.

No. 30 — **Legal Matters:** Legal advice, lawyer, judge, procurer.

No. 31 — **Short Illness:** The court case affects health; deciding for a treatment or medication.

No. 32 — **Grief and Sorrow:** The lawsuit brings a lot of worries, deceived by a judgment, unsolved legal matters.

No. 33 — **Murky Thoughts:** Feeling guilty and anxious, depression caused by a court case, negative thoughts, painful thoughts.

No. 34 — **Occupation:** Judge, lawyer, procurer, working for the authority, a legal job.

No. 35 — **A Long Road:** Slow procedure, a long-term decision, a court case in a distant place, the verdict will take a long time.

No. 36 — **Hope, Big Water:** Hoping for a fair judgment, meditate before making any decision, self-reflection.

A REAL READING FOR
THE COURT CARD

$\mathcal{W}$hen I am doing a Grand Tableau and have specific questions, I often activate some cards that represent the issue I am inquiring about. This time I activated 23 The Court card, as my question was about an administrative procedure. I'd applied for a passport renewal, and the lady told me that I should get it in three weeks; three weeks later, the passport was not ready, as everything is done in France and then transferred to the island. I'd already signed up for a workshop, and my passport was essential for my travel.

In the Grand Tableau, I located the card No. 23 The Court (thereby activating it) and paid attention to the card before, after, on the top, and above (like in a cross formation, 23 The Court card in the center). No. 7 A Pleasant Letter showed that they had received my application, that the procedure was taking longer than expected with 35 A Long Road. No. 22 A Military tells me that things are in order, and 10 A Journey card on the right confirmed that it was on its way, and that I will be traveling soon, certified by the 1 Main Male at the right of the 10 A Journey card (the male querent will be traveling).

35 A Long Road
7 A Pleasant Letter + 23 The Court + 10 A Journey + 1 Main Male
22 A Military

NO. 24
THE THIEVERY

Keywords
Bad Intention, Loss, Fraud, Theft, Something Taken Away

Something is being taken from you; someone is not honest in his action. The Thievery is a card of warning and asks you to watch your surroundings and your possessions. The nature of the loss not only implies physical items; it can be a friendship, a lover, a relationship, or an opportunity. The closer the card is to No. 23 The Court, No. 22 A Military, or 29 The Prison, the more likely you will recover what was taken from you.

Mantra: That which is mine
always comes back to me.

Influence: Negative

Direction: None

Quick answer: No

Topic card: Loss and fraud

Card No. 24—The Thievery with

No. 1 — **Main Male:** The male querent has lost something, the male querent recovers what he had lost, the male querent is facing or is involved in a fraud.

No. 2 — **Main Female:** The female querent has lost something, the female querent recovers what she had lost, the female querent is facing or is involved in a fraud.

No. 3 — **Marriage:** A fraudulent wedding, one of the partners has a secret, lack of honesty, one of them is playing a role.

No. 4 — **A Meeting:** A dangerous meeting, being robbed during a celebration.

No. 5 — **The Good Lord:** The older male has lost something, the older male recovers what he had lost, the older male is facing or is involved in a fraud.

No. 6 — **The Good Lady:** The older female has lost something, the older female recovers what she had lost, the older female is facing or is involved in a fraud.

No. 7 — **A Pleasant Letter:** A lost document, a false statement, a negative letter, a fraudulent letter, credit card fraud.

No. 8 — **False Person:** Dangerous person, a fraud, a theft, an abuser, a fugitive, a recidivist.

No. 9 — **A Change:** Changes are kept secret, being robbed while relocating, a change brings along some losses.

No. 10 — **A Journey:** A clandestine trip, risk of being robbed during travel, car loss, traveling to a fraud, driving a fraud.

No. 11 — **Lot of Money:** Money is stolen, money is lost, a financial fraud.

No. 12 — **A Rich Girl:** Something or someone was taken away from the rich girl, and the thief escaped.

No. 13 — **A Rich Man:** Recovering a lost object, the thief is caught, a luxurious item is stolen.

No. 14 — **Sad News:** Burden is over, end of grief, a correspondence is lost.

No. 15 — **Success in Love:** A secret love, losing a lover, infidelity, untrusting.

No. 16 — **His Thoughts:** Secret plan, planning a holdup, unfair intention.

No. 17 — **A Gift:** Secret gift, a lost gift, risk of kidnapping, a thief visits.

No. 18 — **Small Child:** Recovering a lost object; the thief is caught.

No. 19 — **A Funeral:** Keeping a death secret, burying stolen things, identify usurpation, definitive loss.

No. 20 — **The House:** Losing a house, family secret, burglars, unsafe house, a thief among the family.

No. 21 — **The Living Room:** Loss of intimacy, burglars, unsafe apartment, a thief among the family.

No. 22 — **A Military:** Corrupt officer, the police arrest the thief, the stolen items are recovered by the police.

No. 23 — **The Court:** A falsified document, fraud in the administration, getting a reward through a fraudulent act.

No. 25 — **High Honours:** Recognition and fame earned through doubtful manners, the acknowledgment is taken away, identity theft.

No. 26 — **Big Luck:** Financial fraud, fortune earned through treachery, misappropriation of funds, financial scandal.

No. 27 — **Unexpected Money:** Unexpected problem, money loss, a fraudulent middle-aged woman.

No. 28 — **Expectation:** Find out about a fraud, expecting trickery; dishonest middle-aged woman is up to something.

No. 29 — **The Prison:** The thief is arrested, a fraud leads to imprisonment, the fraud is discovered.

No. 30 — **Legal Matters:** Legal papers are lost, seeking legal advice, lawyer involved in a fraud, the thief's lawyer.

No. 31 — **Short Illness:** A recovery, the disease disappeared, a remission, the pain is over.

No. 32 — **Grief and Sorrow:** Unsolved problem, the loss brings more sorrow, a secret provokes great sorrow.

No. 33 — **Murky Thoughts:** A feeling of injustice, fear of secrets, oppression, a threat.

No. 34 — **Occupation:** Losing a job, thieves at work, secret at work, secretly working, undercover.

No. 35 — **A Long Road:** Long-term loss, distance is reduced, thief from a different location.

No. 36 — **Hope, Big Water:** Losing hope, misplaced hope and faith, a psychic scam, a religious fraud.

THE THIEVERY CARD IN A READING

*L*ike the 23 Mice card in the Lenormand oracle, 24 The Thievery is a card of loss, where something is misplaced or taken away. Its proximity with the querent's card will tell if what was stolen will be recovered. See page xx for a table of equivalence for the Kipper and the Lenormand, both very close but distinctively different. If you are used to reading the Lenormand, then reading Kipper cards will be a piece of cake!

HIGH HONOURS

Keywords

*Recognition, Fame, Reward, Praise, Reputation, Success,
Award, Study, Education, Retirement*

High Honours is one of the good cards you want to see in your reading; it talks about success, recognition, praise, and reputation. It shows how hard you have been working toward your goals, and now these efforts are paying off, and everyone can see it.

Expect good things to happen!

Mantra: I am acknowledged for my talents.

Influence: Positive

Direction: None

Quick answer: Yes

Topic card: Study and education

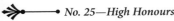

Card No. 25—The High Honours with

No. 1 —   **Main Male:** The male querent is successful; the time has come for him to be acknowledged and rewarded. A time of great success.

No. 2 —   **Main Female:** The female querent is successful; the time has come for her to be acknowledged and rewarded. A time of great success.

No. 3 —   **Marriage:** A good contract, wedding expenses, a contract pays a little, a little money for the couple.

No. 4 —   **A Meeting:** An expected bonus for the group, a refund, small profit for the group.

No. 5 —   **The Good Lord:** The older male is successful; the time has come for him to be acknowledged and rewarded. A time of great success.

No. 6 —   **The Good Lady:** The older female is successful; the time has come for her to be acknowledged and rewarded. A time of great success.

No. 7 —   **A Pleasant Letter:** Unexpected correspondence, a refund, coupons, discount code.

No. 8 —   **False Person:** Dealing with cunning people, a wrong contract, a blocked sum of money.

No. 9 —   **A Change:** Fame and acknowledgment bring a change, a change leads to success, a positive change.

No. 10 —   **A Journey:** Successful travel, a trip to a ceremony, a graduation, rewarded, or winning a car.

No. 11 —   **Lot of Money:** A bonus, a raise, a valuable prize, raising your standards.

No. 12 —   **A Rich Girl:** The younger female is successful; the time has come for her to be acknowledged and rewarded. A time of great success.

No. 13 —   **A Rich Man:** The young male is successful; the time has come for him to be acknowledged and rewarded. A time of great success.

No. 14 —   **Sad News:** False nomination; sad news is acknowledged.

No. 15 —   **Success in Love:** Love of school, love of education, successful completion, love at last, rewarding love life.

No. 16 —   **His Thoughts:** A discovery, an objective, targeted milestone and goals, elevated thoughts.

No. 17 —   **A Gift:** Receiving an award, a diplomat, rewarding someone with a gift.

No. 18 —   **Small Child:** Known child, recognizing an illegitimate child, a successful child, a rewarded child, a talented child.

No. 19 —   **A Funeral:** A glorious funeral, a rejected award, a blocked reward, glory and fame after death.

No. 20 — **The House:** Consulting a housing expert, a real-estate agency, family therapy.

No. 21 — **The Living Room:** Consulting a housing expert, a real-estate agency, family therapy, a sex expert.

No. 22 — **A Military:** Legal advice, lawyer, judge, procurer.

No. 23 — **The Court:** Legal papers are lost, seeking legal advice, lawyer involved in a fraud, the thief's lawyer.

No. 24— **The Thievery:** Recognition and fame earned through doubtful manners, the acknowledgment is taken away, identity theft.

No. 26 — **Big Luck:** Financial reward, complete success, a winning combination, a happy retirement.

No. 27 — **Unexpected Money:** Retired middle-aged woman, lucrative contract, professional success.

No. 28 — **Expectation:** Respected middle-aged woman, high expectation, patience paid off, successful issue.

No. 29 — **The Prison:** Famous building, success provokes loneliness, a hospital with good reputation, a golden cage.

No. 30 — **Legal Matters:** Successful therapy, successful legal advisor, successful lawyer, successful expert.

No. 31 — **Short Illness:** Problem at school, stressful study, a cure is found.

No. 32 — **Grief and Sorrow:** Studying hard, making an effort, known as an addict, a wrong situation, success leads to stress.

No. 33 — **Murky Thoughts:** A fear of success, feeling undeserving, negative thinking.

No. 34 — **Occupation:** A high position, a teacher, an expert, reaching the peak of a career.

No. 35 — **A Long Road:** Long-term success, long studies, studying abroad, your success is abroad.

No. 36 — **Hope, Big Water:** Spiritual education, highly intuitive abilities, wish and hope fulfilled.

Shine like the whole Universe is yours.

—RUMI

NO. 26
BIG LUCK

Keywords

**Blessing, Windfall, Satisfaction, Happy Ending,
Abundance, Luck, Fortune**

The best card you can get in a reading!

The Big Luck card is an indication that all is well, things are improving, and Lady Fortune is with you, pouring her cornucopia of abundance upon you. The Big Luck infuses the surrounding cards with her positiveness and repels away their negative energy.

Mantra: Success and achievement
are natural outcomes for me.

Influence: Positive

Direction: None

Quick answer: Yes

Topic card: Blessings

Card No. 26—Big Luck with

No. 1 — **Main Male:** The male querent is lucky; he can expect happy outcome and lots of success in his ventures.

No. 2 — **Main Female:** The female querent is lucky; she can expect happy outcomes and lots of success in her ventures.

No. 3 — **Marriage:** A successful couple, a lucky union, a blessed marriage, a happy ending.

No. 4 — **A Meeting:** A lucky encounter, a happy meeting, being in good company, a blessed ceremony.

No. 5 — **The Good Lord:** The older male is lucky; he can expect happy outcomes and lots of success in his ventures.

No. 6 — **The Good Lady:** The older female is successful; the time has come for her to be acknowledged and rewarded. A time of success.

No. 7 — **A Pleasant Letter:** A message promises great fortune, a positive turn, exceptional news, an important document.

No. 8 — **False Person:** A blessing in disguise, a protection against jealousy and manipulation, false people are driven away.

No. 9 — **A Change:** Lucky change, happy turn, happy outcome, a blessed change, an epiphany, very positive.

No. 10 — **A Journey:** A great car, a blessed journey, a fortunate trip.

No. 11 — **Lot of Money:** Wealth, fortune, prosperity, financial blessings; you are a good friend with money.

No. 12 — **A Rich Girl:** The young male is lucky; he can expect happy outcomes and lots of success in his ventures.

No. 13 — **A Rich Man:** The young female is lucky; she can expect happy outcomes and lots of success in her ventures.

No. 14 — **Sad News:** A sad situation is handled with care, turning a negative to a positive, tears are shed away—things are getting better.

No. 15 — **Success in Love:** Middle-aged lover, expected partner, expected declaration, expected romance.

No. 16 — **His Thoughts:** One's own expectation, one's own plans, an expected idea.

No. 17 — **A Gift:** Expected gift, middle-aged woman visits, what was expected and awaited is finally here.

No. 18 — **Small Child:** The querent is patient and has strong desires; the next card will say what kind of expectation he may have.

No. 19 — **A Funeral:** A blessed change, a positive termination, an amazing transformation, a blessed funeral.

No. 20 — **The House:** A casino, a gambling house, a successful family, lucky family, fortunate home.

No. 21 — **The Living Room:** A successful family, lucky family, valuable intimacy, personal happiness, one's own luck.

No. 22 — **A Military:** Self-discipline is paying off; the person in uniform is happy.

No. 23 — **The Court:** A fair decision, a blessed verdict, happy outcome, a happy end.

No. 24 — **The Thievery:** Financial fraud, fortune earned through treachery, misappropriation of funds, financial scandal.

No. 25 — **High Honours:** Financial reward, complete success, a winning combination, a happy retirement.

No. 27 — **Unexpected Money:** A financial windfall, unexpected income, unexpected piece of good fortune.

No. 28 — **Expectation:** Expected happy conclusion, acknowledging the blessing, in a state of gratitude.

No. 29 — **The Prison:** Freedom, you are protected, end of isolation and stagnation.

No. 30 — **Legal Matters:** A helpful intervention of a therapist, legal advisor, lawyer, expert.

No. 31 — **Short Illness:** A return to a normal state of health; the situation is healed.

No. 32 — **Grief and Sorrow:** A solution is found, solving past issues, an encouragement.

No. 33 — **Murky Thoughts:** Positive thoughts, overcoming fear, being able to manage stress.

No. 34 — **Occupation:** A blessed job, an amazing career, fortunate position, work provides satisfaction.

No. 35 — **A Long Road:** Long-term success, a time of contentment, a blessing on its way.

No. 36 — **Hope, Big Water:** Spiritual education, highly intuitive abilities, blessed for a long time, wish and hope fulfilled.

BIG LUCK IN A READING

I must admit that No. 26 Big Luck card is my favorite card in the Kipper, and I'm sure it will be yours too. In a Grand Tableau, when the No. 26 Big Luck appears next to the No. 1 Main Male or No. 2 Main Female, it announces that troubles are over and solutions are found. On the other hand, if the Big Luck is afar, his luck and success are inaccessible for now. In terms of position, if the Big Luck appears after a series of negative cards, you can count on your lucky star, as everything will be successfully handled. Furthermore, if a series of negative cards appear after the Big Luck, it's a warning: pay attention, and call upon heavenly help to assist you in your troubles. Again, I want to point out that a reading is rather empowering than fatalistic—every problem has its solution, and with the help of the cards we can obtain this precious help and act accordingly.

NO. 27
UNEXPECTED MONEY

Keywords

Surprising, Unexpected, Profit, Small Sum of Money, Cash, Refund,
Middle-Aged Woman, Unexpected Bonus

This card predicts an unexpected gain!

Most of the time this gain is monetary; the amount is smaller than card No. 11 Lot of Money. It stands for profit, small surprise, or a refund, giving a positive boost to your actual financial situation.

The closer this card is to the 1 Main Male or male seeker, the better it is and the sooner the money will come. Traditionally, the Unexpected Money talks about a middle-aged man, but we know that genders are mutable in card readings.

Mantra: I allow the Universe to bless me in surprising ways.

Influence: Positive

Direction: None

Quick answer: Yes

Topic card: Money

Card No. 27—Unexpected Money with

No. 1 — **Main Male:** A windfall, contract well negotiated is now paying off, unexpected happy surprise, a refund for the male seeker.

No. 2 — **Main Female:** A windfall, contract well negotiated is now paying off, unexpected happy surprise, a refund for the female seeker.

No. 3 — **Marriage:** A successful couple, a lucky union, a blessed marriage, a happy ending.

No. 4 — **A Meeting:** A lucky encounter, a happy meeting, being in good company, a blessed ceremony.

No. 5 — **The Good Lord:** A windfall, contract well negotiated is now paying off, unexpected happy surprise, a refund for the older male.

No. 6 — **The Good Lady:** A windfall, contract well negotiated is now paying off, unexpected happy surprise, a refund for the female seeker.

No. 7 — **A Pleasant Letter:** A message promises great fortune, a positive turn, exceptional news, an important document.

No. 8 — **False Person:** A blessing in disguise, a protection against jealousy and manipulation, false people are driven away.

No. 9 — **A Change:** A change brings money, a financial windfall, contracts well negotiated pay off, unexpected happy surprise.

No. 10 — **A Journey:** A trip brings up some money, traveling for a negotiation, unexpected happy journey, traveling with a middle-aged woman.

No. 11 — **Lot of Money:** Unexpected money, money for a middle-aged woman, payment comes unexpectedly.

No. 12 — **A Rich Girl:** A windfall, contract well negotiated is now paying off, unexpected happy surprise, a refund for the younger male.

No. 13 — **A Rich Man:** A windfall, contract well negotiated is now paying off, unexpected happy surprise, a refund for the younger female.

No. 14 — **Sad News:** Negative news for a middle-aged woman; a raise or payment is rejected.

No. 15 — **Success in Love:** Middle-aged lover, unexpected love, unexpected feelings.

No. 16 — **His Thoughts:** Pondering new resources, indecisive middle-aged woman.

No. 17 — **A Gift:** Unexpected gift, unexpected visitors, a good bargain.

No. 18 — **Small Child:** The child is financially supported, a surprising child, an unexpected gift.

No. 19 — **A Funeral:** Sudden and unexpected passing, an inheritance, a donation, a middle-aged female passed.

No. 20 — **The House:** Unexpected bills, middle-aged neighbor, unexpected money.

No. 21 — **The Living Room:** Unexpected bills, middle-aged neighbor, purchasing an apartment or flat.

No. 22 — **A Military:** A windfall, unexpected happy surprise for the person in uniform, interacting with a middle-aged woman.

No. 23 — **The Court:** The verdict implies payment, paying for administrative procedures, receiving a compensation.

No. 24 — **The Thievery:** Unexpected problem, money loss, a fraudulent middle-aged woman.

No. 25 — **High Honours:** Financial reward, complete success, a winning combination, a happy retirement.

No. 26 — **Big Luck:** Financial reward, complete success, a winning combination, a happy retirement.

No. 28 — **Expectation:** A contract to come, expecting the unexpected, two encounters with middle-aged women (persons).

No. 29 — **The Prison:** A reserved middle-aged woman, a bank interest, tax refund, hospital bill.

No. 30 — **Legal Matters:** Legal matters involving a middle-aged person, gain through lawsuit, receiving an indemnity.

No. 31 — **Short Illness:** A sick middle-aged person, unexpected illness.

No. 32 — **Grief and Sorrow:** A big financial problem, unsolved financial crisis, deceived by the money received.

No. 33 — **Murky Thoughts:** Money caused fear, a disillusion, a stressed middle-aged person.

No. 34 — **Occupation:** A raise in salary, a bonus, overtime, unexpected job.

No. 35 — **A Long Road:** Money from abroad, unexpected gain, a surprise is on its way.

No. 36 — **Hope, Big Water:** Unexpected spiritual gift, hoping for a financial gain.

A REAL READING WITH UNEXPECTED MONEY CARD

Colette came for a session, and her question was about work. I activated the No. 34 Occupation card to represent her work. As I dealt the Grand Tableau, I paid special attention to where this activated card fell. No. 34 Occupation card fell on the 27th position of the Grand Tableau at the house of 27 Unexpected Money (I explain the concept of houses beginning on page 231).

I instantly knew that she would be getting a bonus or a raise in salary, so I asked her if she had asked for a raise. With a big smile she replied yes. I'll let you guess the rest.

NO. 28
EXPECTATION

Keywords
Expectancy, Middle-Aged Woman, Patience, Supposition,
Anticipation, Calculation, Wish, Desire

*N*o. 28 Expectation indicates that this is a time of waiting for things to happen. You need to show patience and let things unfold by themselves—don't rush into anything. The combination of surrounding cards will tell you what kind of expectation the person has: Is it a reply for a new apartment, a declaration of love, or the signature of a contract?

Mantra: I expect great things to happen.

Influence: Neutral

Direction: None

Quick answer: Maybe

Topic card: Wishes and desires

Card No. 28—Expectation with

No. 1 —   **Main Male:** The querent is patient and has strong desires; the next card will say what kind of expectation he has.

No. 2 —   **Main Female:** The querent is patient and has strong desires; the next card will say what kind of expectation she has.

No. 3 —   **Marriage:** Expected alliance, expected contract, a patient couple.

No. 4 —   **A Meeting:** Expecting a meeting, a get-together, a party.

No. 5 —   **The Good Lord:** The older male is patient and has strong desires; the next card will say what kind of expectation he has.

No. 6 —   **The Good Lady:** The older female is patient and has strong desires; the next card will say what kind of expectation she has.

No. 7 —   **A Pleasant Letter:** Messages from a middle-aged woman; expecting a call, a letter, a message.

No. 8 —   **False Person:** An enemy has some expectation, someone is watching from afar, negative expectation, wrong expectation.

No. 9 —   **A Change:** An expected change, patiently waiting for a change, waiting for a move, expected relocation.

No. 10 —   **A Journey:** An expected travel, a departure is awaited, traveling with a middle-aged woman.

No. 11 —   **Lot of Money:** A large sum of money is expected, a rich middle-aged woman.

No. 12 —   **A Rich Girl:** The younger female is patient and has strong desires; the next card will say what kind of expectation she has.

No. 13 —   **A Rich Man:** The younger male is patient and has strong desires; the next card will say what kind of expectation he has.

No. 14 —   **Sad News:** Unfulfilled expectation, sad news for a middle-aged woman, things did not turn out in the way expected.

No. 15 —   **Success in Love:** Middle-aged lover, unexpected love, unexpected feelings.

No. 16 —   **His Thoughts:** Pondering new resources, indecisive middle-aged woman.

No. 17 —   **A Gift:** Unexpected gift, unexpected visitors, a good bargain.

No. 18 —   **Small Child:** The child is financially supported, a surprising child, unexpected gift.

No. 19 —   **A Funeral:** Expected death, expected ending, awaited separation, expecting finality.

No. 20 —   **The House:** Presumption between family members, expectation of a house, family anticipation.

No. 21 —   **The Living Room:** Presumption between family members, expectation of a house, family anticipation.

No. 22 — **A Military:** The person in uniform is patient and has strong desires; the next card will say what kind of expectation he has.

No. 23 — **The Court:** An expected decision, an expected verdict, awaited justice, expected judgment.

No. 24 — **The Thievery:** Unexpected problem, money loss, a fraudulent middle-aged woman.

No. 25 — **High Honours:** Respected middle-aged woman, high expectation, patience paid off, successful issue.

No. 26 — **Big Luck:** Expected happy conclusion, acknowledging the blessing, in a state of gratitude.

No. 27 — **Unexpected Money:** Finds out about a fraud, expecting trickery, dishonest middle-aged woman is up to something.

No. 29 — **The Prison:** A reserved middle-aged woman, isolated person, expected blockage, expected standstill.

No. 30 — **Legal Matters:** Expected legal issues, legal matters involving a middle-aged person, a know-it-all type of person.

No. 31 — **Short Illness:** Expecting a recovery, suspecting a disease, a sick middle-aged person.

No. 32 — **Grief and Sorrow:** Expecting the worst, expectation bring sorrow and deception, obsessive behaviors.

No. 33 — **Murky Thoughts:** Expecting the worst, hidden expectation, secret expectation, negative thoughts.

No. 34 — **Occupation:** Expecting a job, expecting a career opportunity, patience with work.

No. 35 — **A Long Road:** Extremely patient, planning things in advance, long-awaited expectation.

No. 36 — **Hope, Big Water:** A seer, a clairvoyant, someone with the gift of sight, you already knew.

Patience is not sitting and waiting; it is foreseeing.
It is looking at the thorn and seeing the rose, looking
at the night and seeing the day.
—RUMI

NO. 29
THE PRISON

Keywords
Hospital, Building, Sanatorium, Jail, Isolation,
Loneliness, Blockage, Standstill

The Prison is a card that represents a building standing tall. It is a card that relates to captivity, imprisonment, isolation, and blockage. Its proximity to the male or female querent shows a time of standstill, where movements are restricted and patience is needed. Happy are we when No. 29 The Prison is next to the No. 24 The Thievery, letting us know that good prevails and that the universal justice is fair.

Mantra: I live my life freely.

Influence: Negative

Direction: None

Quick answer: No

Topic card: Wishes and desires

Card No. 29—The Prison with

No. 1 — **Main Male:** The male querent is restricted in his actions; lonely, locked away, in a correctional facility, standstill, stagnation.

No. 2 — **Main Female:** The female querent is restricted in her actions; lonely, locked away in a correctional facility, standstill, stagnation.

No. 3 — **Marriage:** Trapped in a marriage, an isolated couple.

No. 4 — **A Meeting:** Trapped by a group, a restricted circle of people.

No. 5 — **The Good Lord:** The older male is restricted in his actions; lonely, locked away in a correctional facility, standstill, stagnation.

No. 6 — **The Good Lady:** The older female is restricted in her actions; lonely, locked away in a correctional facility, standstill, stagnation.

No. 7 — **A Pleasant Letter:** A legal prohibition, a blocked message, protection order notice.

No. 8 — **False Person:** An enemy is blocked, the traitor is punished, the false person is alone.

No. 9 — **A Change:** No change happening, transfer to a new jail, a change is blocked.

No. 10 — **A Journey:** Traveling to a prison, a journey leads to imprisonment.

No. 11 — **Lot of Money:** Tax evasion, money blocked, fee from a hospital or sanatorium costs much.

No. 12 — **A Rich Girl:** The younger female is patient and has strong desires; the next card will say what kind of expectation she has.

No. 13 — **A Rich Man:** The younger male is patient and has strong desires; the next card will say what kind of expectation he has.

No. 14 — **Sad News:** Sad message from a prison or hospital, sad news is kept secret.

No. 15 — **Success in Love:** Forbidden love, dangerous relationship, caught in a relationship.

No. 16 — **His Thoughts:** A blocked plan, planning an outbreak, a stagnation, a standstill.

No. 17 — **A Gift:** A blocked gift, visiting a prison or hospital, a gift is kept away.

No. 18 — **Small Child:** Children's hospital, orphanage, a blocked change, a child in difficulty, a lonely child.

No. 19 — **A Funeral:** Set free, end of hospitalization, dying in the hospital, a blocked change.

No. 20 — **The House:** A sanatorium, a rest house, hospice, care center, housebound.

No. 21 — **The Living Room:** A building, a block of apartments, arrest room, specialized hospital.

No. 22 — **A Military:** Hospital worker, prison guard, policeman.

No. 23 — **The Court:** The lawsuit leads to imprisonment, a government decree, an official verdict.

No. 24 — **The Thievery:** The thief is arrested, a fraud leads to imprisonment, the fraud is discovered.

No. 25 — **High Honours:** Famous building, success provokes loneliness, a hospital with good reputation, a golden cage.

No. 26 — **Big Luck:** Freedom, you are protected, end of isolation and stagnation.

No. 27 — **Unexpected Money:** A reserved middle-aged woman, a bank interest, tax refund, hospital bill.

No. 28 — **Expectation:** A reserved middle-aged woman, isolated person, expected blockage, expected standstill.

No. 30 — **Legal Matters:** Court-appointed attorney, seeing a lawyer, seeking expert advice, a serious lawsuit.

No. 31 — **Short Illness:** Illness requires hospitalization, a hospital, a convalescent home, isolated disease or infection.

No. 32 — **Grief and Sorrow:** Unsolved judicial case, addiction, depression, stressful situation, feeling captive.

No. 33 — **Murky Thoughts:** Expecting the worst, deep-seated fear, a dark time, a depression, self-inflicted situation.

No. 34 — **Occupation:** Health worker, caretaker, a forced activity, working in a penitentiary, restricted activity.

No. 35 — **A Long Road:** The captivity will last, a long time of loneliness, an isolated place.

No. 36 — **Hope, Big Water:** A monastery, a place of spiritual retreat, blocked creative talent, psychic abilities are blocked.

Why do you stay in prison,
when the door is so wide open?

—RUMI

NO. 30
LEGAL MATTERS

Keywords

*Expert, Consultant, Adviser, Counselor, Competence,
Lawyer, Magistrate, Procurer*

*N*o. 30 Legal Matters may relate to a court procedure or legal matters relating to disputes or disagreements bringing discord into your life. It can stand for an authoritative statement of fact.

It is also the cards of experts: lawyers, magistrates, procurer, any person who can bring their expertise to help you in your situation. With good cards around, this card is an ally by your side in your time of trouble.

Mantra: I accept helpful
advice and use it wisely.

Influence: Neutral

Direction: None

Quick answer: Maybe

Topic card: Counseling and advice

Card No. 30—Legal Matters with

No. 1 — **Main Male:** The male querent is seeing a lawyer; he is seeking expertise, dealing with legal matters.

No. 2 — **Main Female:** The female querent is seeing a lawyer; she is seeking expertise, dealing with legal matters.

No. 3 — **Marriage:** Marriage counselor, couple therapy, divorce lawyer.

No. 4 — **A Meeting:** Group therapy, a gathering of experts, lodging a complaint against a group.

No. 5 — **The Good Lord:** The older male is seeing a lawyer; he is seeking expertise, dealing with legal matters.

No. 6 — **The Good Lady:** The older female is seeing a lawyer; she is seeking expertise, dealing with legal matters.

No. 7 — **A Pleasant Letter:** Legal document, letter from an attorney, notice of litigation.

No. 8 — **False Person:** False lawyer, wrong expertise, incorrect advice, a scam.

No. 9 — **A Change:** A lawyer brings change through his expertise, a change in legal matters.

No. 10 — **A Journey:** Going to an expert, car seizure, a complaint related to travel or a car.

No. 11 — **Lot of Money:** Paying for a lawyer, financial advisor, fighting for money, money may cause some argument.

No. 12 — **A Rich Girl:** The younger female is seeing a lawyer; she is seeking expertise, dealing with legal matters.

No. 13 — **A Rich Man:** The younger male is seeing a lawyer; he is seeking expertise, dealing with legal matters.

No. 14 — **Sad News:** A disappointing legal notification, negative news from the lawyer.

No. 15 — **Success in Love:** A priest, a pastor, a guru, a love expert, relationship counselor.

No. 16 — **His Thoughts:** A legal decision, mental dispute, pondering advice.

No. 17 — **A Gift:** A positive legal notice, visited by a judicial officer, dealing with inheritance.

No. 18 — **Small Child:** Adopted child, open-minded expert, an inheritance, a young expert.

No. 19 — **A Funeral:** Inheritance or donation, end of hostility, end of a therapy, a verdict, a definitive decision.

No. 20 — **The House:** A sanatorium, in a rest house, hospice, care center, housebound.

No. 21 — **The Living Room:** A building, a block of apartments, arrest room, specialized hospital.

No. 22 — **A Military:** Hospital worker, prison guard, policeman.

No. 23 — **The Court:** The lawsuit leads to imprisonment, a government decree, an official verdict.

No. 24 — **The Thievery:** The thief is arrested, a fraud leads to imprisonment, the fraud is discovered.

No. 25 — **High Honours:** Successful therapy, successful legal advisor, successful lawyer, successful expert.

No. 26 — **Big Luck:** Helpful intervention of a therapist, legal advisor, lawyer, expert.

No. 27 — **Unexpected Money:** Financial reward, complete success, a winning combination, a happy retirement.

No. 28 — **Expectation:** Expected legal issues, legal matters involving a middle-aged person, a know-it-all type of person.

No. 29 — **The Prison:** Court-appointed attorney, seeing a lawyer, seeking expert advice, a serious lawsuit.

No. 31 — **Short Illness:** Seeking a medical advice, a session with a therapist, consulting a doctor.

No. 32 — **Grief and Sorrow:** A desperate legal procedure, legal matters bring sorrow, a desperate situation.

No. 33 — **Murky Thoughts:** Psychotherapy session, feeling like a victim, negative thoughts on legal procedure.

No. 34 — **Occupation:** A labor court, a magistrate, a lawyer, a doctor, or a legal expert.

No. 35 — **A Long Road:** A long legal procedure, a long therapy, a foreign expert.

No. 36 — **Hope, Big Water:** A psychic reader, a therapist, a healer, a priest, a monk.

JUSTICE, LAW, AND PRISON

*K*ipper cards work wonders when it comes to legal procedures and court cases, as the deck contains a myriad of cards that relate to these issues. At the time Kipper cards were created, people in this era were frightened by the Bavarian militia, and therefore people did not want to have issues with the law.

It would be the same case if a divination deck were created during a war. The cards would give insight into things that people would be facing during a bombardment, oppression, captivity, fear, etc. Remember that the cards are not always literal; they can apply to properties, meanings, and attributes with close attention to the context—as the same card will tell a different story with a different layout.

NO. 31
SHORT ILLNESS

Keywords

Disease, Resting, Recovery, Malaise, Stagnation, Forced to Rest, Weakness, Restriction, Under Medication, Treatment

This card came to you as advice to allow yourself the time to rest. It is not the time to hold on to your worries; things can wait till you feel better. Consulting a doctor is advised. Stress and worries may have brought you here, forced you to rest in bed, and restricted you in your action.

Positive cards around it will ensure your health will improve, but negative cards can aggravate what you already have.

Mantra: I allow my body to heal.

Influence: Negative

Direction: None

Quick answer: No

Topic card: Health

Card No. 31—Short Illness with

No. 1 — **Main Male:** The male querent has a weak health condition. Fever, small infection, light depression, need to rest, need to sleep.

No. 2 — **Main Female:** The female querent has a weak health condition. Fever, small infection, light depression, need to rest, need to sleep.

No. 3 — **Marriage:** Unhealthy, unhappy couple. An unhealthy relationship, a short drama going on.

No. 4 — **A Meeting:** Contagious disease, a group of sick people.

No. 5 — **The Good Lord:** The older male has a weak health condition. Fever, small infection, light depression, need to rest, need to sleep.

No. 6 — **The Good Lady:** The older female has a weak health condition. Fever, small infection, light depression, need to rest, need to sleep.

No. 7 — **A Pleasant Letter:** Checkup results, health results, a health catalog or brochure, disrupting communication.

No. 8 — **False Person:** A wrong diagnosis, pretending to be sick, mental illness, being bullied.

No. 9 — **A Change:** A disease changes form, an illness bring up life changes, relocating due to health issues.

No. 10 — **A Journey:** Car sickness, going to a sick person, not feeling good during a trip.

No. 11 — **Lot of Money:** Expensive healthcare; money may cause some illness.

No. 12 — **A Rich Girl:** The young female has a weak health condition. Fever, small infection, light depression, need to rest, need to sleep.

No. 13 — **A Rich Man:** The young male has a weak health condition. Fever, small infection, light depression, need to rest, need to sleep.

No. 14 — **Sad News:** Serious illness, learning that someone is sick, upsetting disease.

No. 15 — **Success in Love:** Sexual disease, a heartbreak, an unhealthy relationship, heart disease.

No. 16 — **His Thoughts:** Mental illness, schizophrenia, paranoia, lack of focus, concentration.

No. 17 — **A Gift:** A cure, visiting a sick person, childhood disease, sick children.

No. 18 — **Small Child:** A sick child, a delay, a blockage, childhood disease, weak child, sleepy child.

No. 19 — **A Funeral:** Depending on the question, it can be an aggravated illness or the end of illness.

No. 20 — **The House:** Home hospitalization, sick family member, stress family, a hereditary disease.

No. 21 —   **The Living Room:** Sick family member, private life is affected, an infirmary, forced to rest.

No. 22 —   **A Military:** A doctor, a therapist, medical advisor; self-discipline is required to heal.

No. 23 —   **The Court:** The court case affects one's health; deciding for a treatment or medication.

No. 24 —   **The Thievery:** Illness requires hospitalization; a hospital, a convalescent home, isolated disease or infection.

No. 25 —   **High Honours:** Problem at school, stressful study, a cure is found.

No. 26 —   **Big Luck:** A return to a normal state of health; the situation is healed.

No. 27 —   **Unexpected Money:** A sick middle-aged person, unexpected illness.

No. 28 —   **Expectation:** Expecting a recovery, suspecting a disease, a sick middle-aged person.

No. 29 —   **The Prison:** Illness requires hospitalization; a hospital, a convalescent home, isolated disease or infection.

No. 30 —   **Legal Matters:** Seeking a medical advice, a session with a therapist, consulting a doctor.

No. 32 —   **Grief and Sorrow:** Deep addiction, deep depression, stressful situation, feeling captive, unable to care for yourself.

No. 33 —   **Murky Thoughts:** Expecting the worst, deep-seated fear, a dark time, a depression, self-inflicted situation.

No. 34 —   **Occupation:** Working in the health sector, a caretaker, inability to work, sick leave.

No. 35 —   **A Long Road:** A chronic condition, a long-term recovery, a long disease.

No. 36 —   **Hope, Big Water:** Hope for a recovery; disease related to body fluid, alternative healing modalities.

A REAL READING WITH
SHORT ILLNESS

*R*ose came to me quite worried with her mom's health and wanted to have some guidance. **I must say here that psychic readings give an overview on one's health situation but never replace the diagnosis and expertise of a doctor. It should not be used for medical treatment plans.** I dealt the Grand Tableau and paid special attention to the first three cards of the draw, as these represent for me what is going on; these cards will flavor the reading. The cards that came up were 31 Short Illness + 16 His Thoughts + 29 The Prison. The cards again are clear that Rose's mom is ill, and this has to do with her mind—a hospitalization is greatly needed. She is the prisoner of her mind, and I instantly get the word "Alzheimer" in my head.

I told everything to Rose, and she confirmed what was shown. It was also a validation of her own suspicions.

Remember to always combine the message of the cards with your intuition; let the cards give you impressions, thoughts, and feelings. They are extensions of your psychic awareness; marry them together, and you will experience the most amazing reading ever.

GRIEF AND SORROW

Keywords
Deception, Unsolved Problems, Desperation,
Grief, Setback, Adversity, Failure

$\mathcal{S}$omeone in your surroundings may try to bully or put pressure on you to do something you do not want to do. Your thoughts may not be clear enough to make a judgment. Worry and frustration are all around you.

With positive cards, the problem finds a solution and can be quickly solved; with more negatively oriented cards, the situation is desperate, and only prayers and positive thoughts can help you overcome the situation.

Mantra: I easily overcome any setback I encounter.

Influence: Negative

Direction: None

Quick answer: No

Topic card: Adversity

Card No. 32—Grief and Sorrow with

No. 1 — **Main Male:** The male querent goes through a difficult time, is in a depression; healing from addiction.

No. 2 — **Main Female:** The female querent goes through a difficult time, is in a depression; healing from addiction.

No. 3 — **Marriage:** The couple is going through a tough time; unresolved marital issues, failed relationship.

No. 4 — **A Meeting:** Social crisis, a healing circle, a meeting failed.

No. 5 — **The Good Lord:** The older male goes through a difficult time, is in a depression; healing from addiction.

No. 6 — **The Good Lady:** The older female querent goes through a difficult time, is in a depression; healing from addiction.

No. 7 — **A Pleasant Letter:** Sad news, fear of a particular message or document, writing about grief, a message of emotional distress.

No. 8 — **False Person:** An enemy is causing much pain through gossip and harassment; fake despair, drama queen.

No. 9 — **A Change:** A trip causes pain, a car brings a lot of worry, a painful trip.

No. 10 — **A Journey:** A trip causes pain, a car brings a lot of worry, a painful trip.

No. 11 — **Lot of Money:** Money causes grief, big money problem, major financial obstacles.

No. 12 — **A Rich Girl:** The younger male goes through a difficult time, is in a depression; healing from addiction.

No. 13 — **A Rich Man:** The young male goes through a difficult time, is in a depression; healing from addiction.

No. 14 — **Sad News:** Life crisis, a hopeless situation, things are getting worse.

No. 15 — **Success in Love:** Life crisis, a hopeless situation, things are getting worse.

No. 16 — **His Thoughts:** Mental harassment, depression, thoughts of the past, obsession.

No. 17 — **A Gift:** Deceiving gift, troublesome visit, a painful gift, painful visit.

No. 18 — **Small Child:** A deceived child, rejected child, abused child, addicted child.

No. 19 — **A Funeral:** Despairing situation, unable to recover from grief, a great deception, painful situation.

No. 20 — **The House:** Family deception, addicted family, family conflict, shaky foundation, unsolved family problem.

No. 21 — **The Living Room:** Unsolved personal problems, private life is in decadence, deceived by private life.

No. 22 — **A Military:** A difficult time to come, problems and difficulties pile up before the person in uniform, a pattern, a depression, an addiction.

No. 23 — **The Court:** The lawsuit brings a lot of worries, deceived by a judgment, unsolved legal matters.

No. 24 — **The Thievery:** Unsolved problem, the loss brings more sorrow, a secret provokes great sorrow.

No. 25 — **High Honours:** Studying hard, making effort, known as an addict, a wrong situation, success leads to stress.

No. 26 — **Big Luck:** A solution is found, solving past issues, an encouragement.

No. 27 — **Unexpected Money:** A big financial problem, unsolved financial crisis, deceived by the money received.

No. 28 — **Expectation:** Expecting the worst, expectation brings sorrow and deception, obsessive behaviors.

No. 29 — **The Prison:** Unsolved judicial case, addiction, depression, stressful situation, feeling captive.

No. 30 — **Legal Matters:** A desperate legal procedure, legal matters bring sorrow, a desperate situation.

No. 31 — **Short Illness:** Deep addiction, deep depression, stressful situation, feeling captive, unable to care for yourself.

No. 33 — **Murky Thoughts:** Paralyzing grief, fear of failure, hidden deception, secret addiction.

No. 34 — **Occupation:** Trouble with colleagues, bullying, professional crisis, problem at work.

No. 35 — **A Long Road:** Longtime problem, deep-rooted depression, problem stays unsolved.

No. 36 — **Hope, Big Water:** Loss of hope, deceived by religion and spirituality, spiritually disoriented.

GRIEF AND SORROW
IN A READING

*T*his is a David and Goliath type of card, where the querent had small means to affront adversity. It's also a card that reminds you that if you target your goal, nothing can stop you from attaining it.

The tools to help you attain your goals are prayers and a positive attitude to your situation. Nothing is written in stone; I rather believe that it's written in pencil, and that we have in us the eraser to rewrite the outcome we want to experience. Being positive doesn't mean that you live in denial; it's that you are approaching the situation with a detached perspective.

MURKY THOUGHTS

Keywords
Ego's Voice, Panic, Secrets, Hidden Thoughts, Fear,
Oppression, Deception, Doubts

*T*he Murky Thoughts relate to a state of turbulence, of fear and doubt. The voice of the ego is clearly dragging you down. Remember that it is a state that you can choose to leave by simply changing and shifting the way you think.

Mantra: I choose to think happy thoughts.

Influence: Negative

Direction: None

Quick answer: No

Topic card: Power of the mind

Card No. 33—Murky Thoughts with

No. 1 — **Main Male:** The male querent is in a negative mood; he is lost in fear; drama queen, negative thinking.

No. 2 — **Main Female:** The female querent is in a negative mood; she is lost in fear; drama queen, negative thinking.

No. 3 — **Marriage:** The couple has fearful thoughts, hidden secrets, doubts, and unsolved issues.

No. 4 — **A Meeting:** Avoiding social events, a resistor to social life.

No. 5 — **The Good Lord:** The older male is in a negative mood; he is lost in fear; drama queen, negative thinking.

No. 6 — **The Good Lady:** The older female is in a negative mood; she is lost in fear; drama queen, negative thinking.

No. 7 — **A Pleasant Letter:** A message of emotional distress, a message brought out a lot of doubt and negative thoughts.

No. 8 — **False Person:** An enemy is causing much pain through gossip and harassment; fake despair, drama queen, someone is pulling your morality down.

No. 9 — **A Change:** Fear of change, not wanting to move or relocate, depressed about an imminent departure.

No. 10 — **A Journey:** Fear of driving, not wanting to travel, depressed about an imminent departure.

No. 11 — **Lot of Money:** Existential fear, fear of money, negative thought about money, feeling undeserving.

No. 12 — **A Rich Girl:** The younger female is in a negative mood; she is lost in fear; drama queen, negative thinking.

No. 13 — **A Rich Man:** The younger male is in a negative mood; he is lost in fear; drama queen, negative thinking.

No. 14 — **Sad News:** Negative feedback, news brings fear and discouragement.

No. 15 — **Success in Love:** Fear of love, disappointment, fear of being loved and to love.

No. 16 — **His Thoughts:** Suspicions and doubts, negative thoughts, deception, overestimation.

No. 17 — **A Gift:** Unwanted visit, suspicious gift, fearful visitation, fearful children.

No. 18 — **Small Child:** The small child is lost in fear, a role play, a drama.

No. 19 — **A Funeral:** Anxiety, depression, grief is overwhelming, negative thoughts, painful thoughts.

No. 20 — **The House:** Anxious and depressive family. Family with secrets, not sharing their thoughts, a frightened family.

No. 21 — **The Living Room:** Anxiety about one's private life; is worried about an apartment, has private secrets.

No. 22 — **A Military:** Always sees the glass half empty, like to keep himself worrying with dark thoughts.

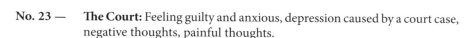

No. 23 — **The Court:** Feeling guilty and anxious, depression caused by a court case, negative thoughts, painful thoughts.

No. 24 — **The Thievery:** A feeling of injustice, fear of secrets, an oppression, a threat.

No. 25 — **High Honours:** A fear of success, feeling undeserving, negative thinking.

No. 26 — **Big Luck:** Positive thoughts, overcoming fear, being able to manage stress.

No. 27 — **Unexpected Money:** Money caused fear; a disillusion, a stressed middle-aged person.

No. 28 — **Expectation:** Expecting the worst, hidden expectation, secret expectation, negative thoughts.

No. 29 — **The Prison:** Expecting the worst, deep-seated fear, a dark time, a depression, self-inflicted situation.

No. 30 — **Legal Matters:** Psychotherapy session, feeling like a victim, negative thought on legal procedure.

No. 31 — **Short Illness:** Expecting the worst, deep-seated fear, a dark time, a depression, self-inflicted situation.

No. 32 — **Grief and Sorrow:** Paralyzing grief, fear of failure, hidden deception, secret addiction.

No. 34 — **Occupation:** Trouble with colleagues, bullying, professional crisis, problem at work.

No. 35 — **A Long Road:** Longtime problem, deep-rooted depression, problem stays unsolved, a pattern, bipolarity.

No. 36 — **Hope, Big Water:** Lost of hope, deceived by religion and spirituality, spiritually disoriented.

Do you know what you are?
You are a manuscript of a divine letter.
You are a mirror reflecting a noble face.
This universe is not outside you.
Look inside yourself, everything that you want,
you are already that.

—RUMI

NO. 34
OCCUPATION

Keywords

*Job, Career, Hard Work, Industrious, Ready for Action,
Making Things Happen*

$\mathcal{N}$o 34 Occupation is a card that represents what you do for a living. It can also stand for things that keep you busy—it can be a passion, a hobby that really asks for dedication.

As always, the surrounding cards will provide more clarity. Positive cards would bless the working atmosphere whereas the negative ones would add tension and challenge.

Mantra: I love my job.

Influence: Neutral

Direction: None

Quick answer: Maybe

Topic card: Work and career

Card No. 34—Occupation with

No. 1 — **Main Male:** Hardworking, motivated, ambitious man; a job offer.

No. 2 — **Main Female:** Hardworking, motivated, ambitious woman; a job offer.

No. 3 — **Marriage:** The couple works together, a business deal, a fusion of enterprise.

No. 4 — **A Meeting:** Being married to his career, a boyfriend/girlfriend can be found in the working environment.

No. 5 — **The Good Lord:** Hardworking, motivated, ambitious elderly man; a job offer.

No. 6 — **The Good Lady:** Hardworking, motivated, ambitious elderly woman; a job offer.

No. 7 — **A Pleasant Letter:** Work-related document, a writer, a poet, a blogger, someone who express himself through creative writing.

No. 8 — **False Person:** Traitor in the workplace, manipulation in the work environment, unfaithful colleague.

No. 9 — **A Change:** Work involves mobility, change in career; changes occurring in the workplace with boss and colleagues.

No. 10 — **A Journey:** Work involves mobility, driving to work, car salesman, working in the tourism industry.

No. 11 — **Lot of Money:** Money through work, a raise in salary, good salary, working with money, investor.

No. 12 — **A Rich Girl:** Hardworking, motivated, ambitious young woman; a job offer, a banker.

No. 13 — **A Rich Man:** Hardworking, motivated, ambitious young man; a job offer, a banker.

No. 14 — **Sad News:** Sad news from work, unhealthy working environment, receiving a refusal.

No. 15 — **Success in Love:** Love of work, doing what you love, successful career, loyal to duty.

No. 16 — **His Thoughts:** Work plans, career plans, work preoccupation, psychologist.

No. 17 — **A Gift:** A nanny, working with children, flower shop, toy shop, gift shop.

No. 18 — **Small Child:** Working with children, a hard-working child, small job, teacher, caretaker.

No. 19 — **A Funeral:** Retirement, career reconversion, getting fired, end-of-a-job contract, working for a funeral home.

No. 20 — **The House:** Home office, working from home, freelance worker, safe work, working with family.

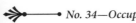

No. 21 — **The Living Room:** Home office, working from home, freelance worker, housekeeping, working with family.

No. 22 — **A Military:** Hardworking, motivated, disciplined, and ambitious man.

No. 23 — **The Court:** Judge, lawyer, procurer, working for the authority, a legal job.

No. 24 — **The Thievery:** Losing a job, thieves at work, secret at work, secretly working.

No. 25 — **High Honours:** A high position, a teacher, an expert, reaching the peak of a career.

No. 26 — **Big Luck:** A blessed job, an amazing career, fortunate position, work provides satisfaction.

No. 27 — **Unexpected Money:** A raise in salary, a bonus, overtime, unexpected job.

No. 28 — **Expectation:** Expecting a job, expecting a career opportunity, patience with work.

No. 29 — **The Prison:** An imposed or forced activity, working under surveillance. Health worker, caretaker, a forced activity, working in a penitentiary, restricted activity.

No. 30 — **Legal Matters:** A labor court, a magistrate, a lawyer, a doctor, a legal expert.

No. 31 — **Short Illness:** Working in the health sector, a caretaker, unable to work, sick leaves.

No. 32 — **Grief and Sorrow:** Trouble with colleagues, bullying, professional crisis, problem at work.

No. 33 — **Murky Thoughts:** Trouble with colleagues, bullying, professional crisis, problem at work.

No. 35 — **A Long Road:** Long-term job, a job position in a different state or country, longtime occupation, working at a distance.

No. 36 — **Hope, Big Water:** Working in the esoteric business: psychic, intuitive; a vocation, an artist.

NO. 35
A LONG ROAD

Keywords

*Long Distance, Avenues and Trees, In a Different Location,
Paths, Long-Term Plans, Patience*

A Long Road talks about things happening for the long term and at a long distance, both geographically and in time. The surrounding cards will give more clues about the direction. It's a card that tells you to have patience, as things may be happening behind the scene but are not yet visible for you.

Mantra: Everything happens at the right time.

Influence: Neutral

Direction: None

Quick answer: Maybe

Topic card: Time

Card No. 35—A Long Road with

No. 1 — **Main Male:** Traveling to a distant destination; patience—things will not happen now for the male querent.

No. 2 — **Main Female:** Traveling to a distant destination; patience—things will not happen now for the female querent.

No. 3 — **Marriage:** Long-distance relationship; they have been waiting patiently for this marriage to happen, long-term commitment.

No. 4 — **A Meeting:** A gathering and reunion held in another state or country, long-term commitment.

No. 5 — **The Good Lord:** Patient elderly man, a good man from afar.

No. 6 — **The Good Lady:** Patient elderly woman, a good woman from afar.

No. 7 — **A Pleasant Letter:** A letter from afar, a message that asks for one's patience.

No. 8 — **False Person:** An enemy from afar, an enemy patiently waiting, a plan of revenge.

No. 9 — **A Change:** Moving/relocating to a distant destination; patience—things will not happen now.

No. 10 — **A Journey:** Traveling to a foreign country, a long trip, a long distance, a faraway place.

No. 11 — **Lot of Money:** Long-term investment, money at a distance, money out of reach.

No. 12 — **A Rich Girl:** Traveling to a distant destination; patience—things will not happen now for the younger female.

No. 13 — **A Rich Man:** Traveling to a distant destination; patience—things will not happen now for the younger male.

No. 14 — **Sad News:** Discomfort, bad news coming from far, sad situation that persists.

No. 15 — **Success in Love:** Happily ever after, eternal love, long-distance relationship, forever loyal, long-term happiness.

No. 16 — **His Thoughts:** Long-term plans, thinking things in advance, long-term goals.

No. 17 — **A Gift:** A gift comes from far away, a visitor from far away, prolonged visit.

No. 18 — **Small Child:** A new project on its way, showing a lot of patience, a foreign child, baby steps.

No. 19 — **A Funeral:** Slow death, a slow change, slow motion, a fateful change.

No. 20 — **The House:** A secondary residence far away, family members living far away, acquiring a house will take time.

No. 21 — **The Living Room:** A secondary residence far away, close family members living far away, acquiring an apartment will take time.

No. 22 — **A Military:** The person in uniform is patient in his action and waits for the perfect time to act.

No. 23 — **The Court:** Slow procedure, a long-term decision, a court case in a distant place, the verdict will take a long time.

No. 24 — **The Thievery:** Long-term loss, distance is reduced, thief from a different location.

No. 25 — **High Honours:** Long-term success, long studies, studying abroad, your success is abroad.

No. 26 — **Big Luck:** Money from abroad, unexpected gain, a surprise on its way.

No. 27 — **Unexpected Money:** Money from abroad, unexpected gain, a surprise on its way.

No. 28 — **Expectation:** Extremely patient, planning things in advance, long-awaited expectation.

No. 29 — **The Prison:** The captivity will last, a long time of loneliness, an isolated place.

No. 30 — **Legal Matters:** A long legal procedure, a long therapy, a foreign expert.

No. 31 — **Short Illness:** A chronic condition, a long-term recovery, a slow and progressive disease.

No. 32 — **Grief and Sorrow:** Longtime problem, deep-rooted depression, problem stays unsolved.

No. 33 — **Murky Thoughts:** Longtime problem, deep-rooted depression, problem stays unsolved, a pattern, bipolarity.

No. 34 — **Occupation:** Long-term job, a job position in a different state or country, longtime occupation, working at a distance.

No. 36 — **Hope, Big Water:** Overseas travel, migration, a spiritual trip, past life.

NO. 36
HOPE, BIG WATER

Keywords

*Hopes, Wishes, Dreams, Foreign Places, Psychic Awareness,
Spirituality, Exoteric*

*H*ope, Big Water represents the hopes, dreams, and wishes you want fulfilled.
The card also refers to traveling to foreign countries.

For me, it's a very powerful card as it represents spirituality and intuition;
the cards around it will indicate in which area of life you need to use your
psyche in order to deal with the situation.

Mantra: I am open and receptive
to my psychic gifts.

Influence: Neutral to Positive

Direction: None

Quick answer: Yes

Topic card: Spirituality

Card No. 36—Hope, Big Water with

No. 1 —   **Main Male:** The male querent travels abroad, crossing waters; the event will happen in a foreign land; feeling hopeful, an intuitive.

No. 2 —   **Main Female:** The female querent travels abroad, crossing waters; the event will happen in a foreign land; feeling hopeful, an intuitive.

No. 3 —   **Marriage:** The couple has hope, the couple is spiritually oriented, they have faith in each other.

No. 4 —   **A Meeting:** A fateful meeting, a social group, a group reading, a psychic fair.

No. 5 —   **The Good Lord:** The older man travels abroad, crossing waters; the event will happen in a foreign land; feeling hopeful, an intuitive.

No. 6 —   **The Good Lady:** The older man travels abroad, crossing waters; the event will happen in a foreign land; feeling hopeful, an intuitive.

No. 7 —   **A Pleasant Letter:** A message of hope, boat or cruise tickets, a letter from a foreign country.

No. 8 —   **False Person:** Traveling abroad or immigrating is wrong, a misconception, false hope.

No. 9 —   **A Change:** Hoping for a change, uncertain change, a change in your spiritual beliefs or practice.

No. 10 —   **A Journey:** Great hopes on a journey, a cruise, a meditation journey, a spiritual journey.

No. 11 —   **Lot of Money:** Money comes from abroad, investing in your spirituality, good intuition on money.

No. 12 —   **A Rich Girl:** The young male travels abroad, crossing waters; the event will happen in a foreign land; feeling hopeful, an intuitive.

No. 13 —   **A Rich Man:** The young male travel abroad, crossing waters; the event will happen in a foreign land; feeling hopeful, an intuitive.

No. 14 —   **Sad News:** Sad news from abroad, hopeless situation, feeling overwhelmingly sad.

No. 15 —   **Success in Love:** A spiritual or religious wedding, sea lover, past-life lover, love gives much hope.

No. 16 —   **His Thoughts:** An intuition, clairsentience, one's own hope, spiritually minded.

No. 17 —   **A Gift:** Gift of intuition, gifted a voyage or cruise, a gift brings hope to the receiver, an offering.

No. 18 —   **Small Child:** A gifted child, child with psychic abilities or any kind of artistic talent.

No. 19 —   **A Funeral:** Mediumship, loved ones in heaven, end of hope, a spiritual death, near-death experience.

No. 20 —   **The House:** Spiritual house, spiritual family, house near the waters, a foreign secondary residence.

No. 21 —   **The Living Room:** Sacred space, an apartment by the waters, someone has hope regarding an apartment.

No. 22 —   **A Military:** The person in uniform is gifted; he may have psychic abilities or any kind of artistic talent.

No. 23 —   **The Court:** Hoping for a fair judgment, meditate before taking any decision, self-reflection.

No. 24 —   **The Thievery:** Losing hope, misplaced hope and faith, a psychic scam, a religious fraud.

No. 25 —   **High Honours:** Spiritual education, highly intuitive abilities, wish and hope fulfilled.

No. 26 —   **Big Luck:** Spiritual education, highly intuitive abilities, a longtime blessing, wish and hope fulfilled.

No. 27 —   **Unexpected Money:** Unexpected spiritual gift, hoping for a financial gain.

No. 28 —   **Expectation:** A seer, a clairvoyant, someone with the gift of sight, you already knew.

No. 29 —   **The Prison:** A monastery, a place of spiritual retreat, blocked creative talent, psychic abilities are blocked.

No. 30 —   **Legal Matters:** A psychic reader, a therapist, a healer, a priest, a monk.

No. 31 —   **Short Illness:** Hope for a recovery, disease related to body fluid, alternative healing modalities.

No. 32 —   **Grief and Sorrow:** Loss of hope, deceived by religion and spirituality, spiritually disoriented.

No. 33 —   **Murky Thoughts:** Loss of hope, deceived by religion and spirituality, spiritually disoriented.

No. 34 —   **Occupation:** Working in the esoteric business: psychic, intuitive; a vocation, an artist.

No. 35 —   **A Long Road:** Overseas travel, migration, a spiritual trip, past life.

CARD

REVERSALS

From my perspective of reading the Kipper cards, I never read reversed cards. Even if they happen to appear as such, I would just flip them upright and carry on with the reading. When it comes to learning the system, the 36 cards have enough information and stories to tell; you don't need another layer of 36. Imagine how overwhelming and confusing it might be when you would have to deal the Grand Tableau and its Houses.

In Tarot, reversals work wonderfully, but not in Kipper; the two systems are distinctive, and I prefer to keep them separate. One can successfully use Tarot in conjunction with Kipper. I love how Kipper instantly gives a snapshot of the querent's life: his worries, thoughts, expectations, environment, love life, finances, health, and much more. Through my experience with Kipper card reading, I've noticed that with practice the card's messages become increasingly easier, so practice as much as you can and let your skills sharpen.

BASIC

3-CARD

SPREAD

*T*he layout of cards in a pattern is called a card spread. Each position in the spread has a meaning, and there are many different types of spreads, ranging from those that incorporate two cards to spreads that include all 36 Kipper cards. In this section of the book, I will explain card spreads and how to use them.

We will start with the basic and fundamental ones, which are the 3-, 5-, and 9-card spreads that lead to the gigantic Grand Tableau. The 3- and 5-card spreads are also known as "strings." This is where you lay out the cards from left to right in a horizontal line; these strings are usually used to answer one question at a time. It's an easy and fast way to get a clear answer. The center card is always the focus; it represents the situation. The card on the left side describes this focus card, and I see the last or right card as the answer or the punctuation to the reading.

Let's take an example for a better understanding: Jean is divorced and has had difficulty finding a partner. He wanted the cards to give him advice on what he could do to attract someone. After the usual shuffle and cut, I fanned the deck before Jean, asking him to pull three cards randomly with his left hand, the hand of the heart. The cards he pulled were

1 Main Male + 18 Small Child + 15 Success in Love

These cards are very interesting in respect to the context of Jean's question.
First thing I notice is, of course, card No. 1 the Main Male representing
Jean. Jean is tuned into his future in this position. What I can say is that all
his attention is focused on his becoming. No. 18 The Small Child and the
15 Success in Love are behind him in his past, telling me that Jean had been
happy in a relationship and even had children. The Success in Love in the
past gives very small chances for Jean to find a loving relationship, even if
he is focused on his future; the emotional baggage of fatherhood and of a
past loving relationship still affects him. I really want to have additional
insight about his future, so I invited Jean to pull a clarifying card that is
placed on the 1 Main Male card. He pulled card No. 33 Murky Thoughts,
and now I understand better.

What the cards were trying to tell us was that Jean had unfinished business
with a child and ex-wife, and as long as he keeps from resolving those issues,
no serious relationship will come. The 33 Murky Thoughts encourage Jean to
uplift his thoughts, stop the drama, and forgive. Jean could relate to the reading
and admitted that he was still angry with his ex-wife because she cheated on
him, and it was difficult for him when he met someone not to think that she
might do the same thing to him.

THE
5-CARD
CROSS SPREAD

$\mathcal{T}$his is a great spread to analyze a situation; it gives clues to what is going on, where your weakness lies, and your strength. You don't need to have a precise question to use this spread, and this technique will be constantly used in the Grand Tableau reading. The positions 4 and 5 are mutable, as it will depend on the querent's direction, which means the direction of the characters in the card look will be the future, and what is behind their back is the past. Positions 2 and 3 are fixed, whereas position 1 can be the significator that you put in a cross. (I call that crossing the querent or crossing the key card.) Here is the placement and their meaning:

1: WHERE YOU ARE AT NOW, THE PRESENT, YOUR QUESTION.

2: WHAT IS OUT OF YOUR REACH, WHAT IS ON YOUR MIND THAT HAS NOT YET MATERIALIZED.

3: WHAT YOU ALREADY HAVE, WHAT YOU HAVE ACHIEVED.

4: WHAT YOU SHOULD SURRENDER, YOUR PAST.

5: WHAT YOU BRING IN, THE FUTURE.

A REAL READING WITH
THE CROSS SPREAD

*F*or this reading example, I choose the story of Evelyn. She came for a reading at a time when she was struggling with her love life. Her uncertainty brought up lot of stress, and she was on the verge of depression and needed guidance.

I wanted the cards to tell where she was now, where she was heading, and what were the energies influencing her. The Cross Spread seems to be the best choice for this reading. As I always do, I shuffled, she cut the cards, and from the top I picked the first five cards and placed them in the pattern of the cross. Here what came up for her:

My Interpretation:

No. 34 Occupation is the center card, showing that Evelyn's love life keeps her very busy; there is lot going on. The 12 A Rich Girl flavors that 34 Occupation card, telling me that Evelyn had always known a comfortable and privileged relationship—youth and carefree is reflected here. No. 22 A Military in the past shows that Evelyn was the dominant one, ruling her relationship as she wished, putting out laws and rules, expecting to be obeyed without discussion. The cause of the problem seemed to be immaturity; she had been rude with her partner, acting like a diva—and now it's enough for him, and he is making Evelyn pay for her attitude. The 31 Short Illness in the mind position shows that the atmosphere is not really the best.

Knowing what is at the heart of the matter, let's investigate more to give Evelyn some practical advice on how she can make things better. For me, the purpose of a reading not only is to get answers; it's also having practical advice that will enable healing.

The 26 Big Luck in the future tells me that the outcome can be a good one. The Big Luck is the most powerful card in the deck, and it talks about blessing, gratitude, fortune, wishes granted, and the best possible outcome. Making a long story short, I told Evelyn that she needs to be grateful for her love life and to stop the diva and military thing. Tell her partner how lucky she is to have him and that she really acknowledges him for everything he does.

She admitted that she had the bad habit of controlling everything and being very demanding. Evelyn promised herself that she would change and put more positivity in her life. I gave her an affirmation repeat for homework: "I release the need to control everything; I am grateful for my love life."

Six month later, Evelyn came for a reading about her work, and she gladly said that life is better since her last session. She had changed her behaviors, and her partner was extremely happy for this change—he'd been a skeptic at first, but now he was a believer.

THE 9-CARD BOX SPREAD

*When you do things from
your soul, you feel a river
moving in you, a joy.*
—RUMI

*T*he 9-card spread, a.k.a. the Box Spread, is one of my favorites. I use it a lot in my private practice, and you will see my countless YouTube videos where I give readings using this spread. I get a lot of information from the cards' interactions. There are many ways to lay down and interpret the Box Spread—the diagram will guide you to the way I lay out the cards.

Meanings of the Positions

Focus card: 1
Past: 6, 4, 8
Present: 2, 1, 3
Future/outcome: 7, 5, 9
Energy/influence: 6, 7, 8, 9
What's on your mind / what weight is heavy: 6, 2, 7
What you are currently dealing with: 4, 1, 5
The lessons learned / what's under control: 8, 3, 9
Indirect influences: 6, 1, 9 and 8, 1, 7
Confirmation: 4, 2, 5, 3
Answer: 9

THE

GRAND

TABLEAU

*E*verything leads to the Grand Tableau! The Grand Tableau (GT) is a French term that means "Big Picture." It's a unique system of divination that uses all 36 cards of the deck at once. I consider the Grand Tableau as a magical map of life that holds a richness of guidance and power.

When I open the cards, the tableau reveals my client's journey, from where he came from, to what landscape he is experiencing at this very moment, and what is about to come for him. The Grand Tableau can recognize or bring to the light hidden influences and patterns that may be blocking the client from progressing and reaching accomplishment.

With the Grand Tableau, you can see what is happening in your love life, finances, career, health, spirituality, family—everything that concerns your life. I use the traditional 9 (cards in a line horizontally) × 4 (cards in a line vertically) formation in my readings (as shown).

Everything that you've been reading from the previous chapters will be used here. I have created a 7-key method that you would utilize to read your Grand Tableau successfully. When I cast a Grand Tableau, I ask my client to cut the cards and focus on what he would like to know; remember that the

GT can reply to several questions at once and also give a sneak peek of other areas of life. I will use diagrams to help me in my explanation, I found that visual examples do leave an imprint in your mind and make things easier to remember. Shuffle your cards and deal them in a 9 × 4 formation, the card faces facing up.

SPECIAL AUTHOR NOTE

The Grand Tableau is for advanced readers. If you are a newbie to Kipper card reading, please don't start with the GT, as you need to get the fundamentals first; master the card meanings, directions, and small spreads and get to know your cards, since this training will help you immensely in your GT. If you start right from here, you will find the system overwhelming and will be discouraged to the point of thinking that Kipper card reading is not for you. And, in truth, Kipper is for everyone who wants to invest the time and discipline.

Let's start the exploration!

7 KEYS TO

UNLOCK

THE GRAND TABLEAU

Key 1
THE FIRST 3 CARDS OF
THE GRAND TABLEAU

These 3 cards open the game and set the theme and tone of the reading. They will talk about what is being brought to the table.

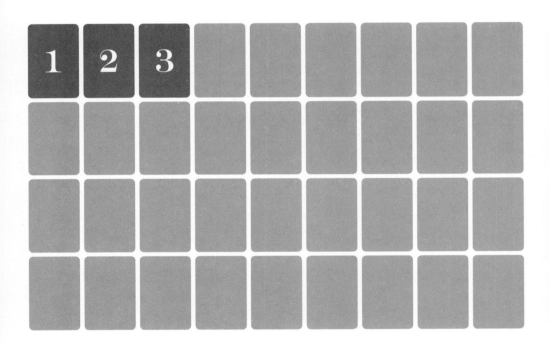

To this point, with practice, you've been mastering the 3-card reading, and here it comes into play.

For instance:

17 A Gift + 36 Hope, Big Water + 25 High Honours

We will be talking about the dream and wish the querent has; his/her aspiration. The reading starts with a very positive note.

Remember to align the meaning of the cards with the context of the question so that the meaning can perfectly match the situation. The Grand Tableau is a collection of small spreads that lead to the grand reading.

Let's move to the next step.

Key 2
WHERE THE SIGNIFICATOR LANDED

Notice where your significator, 1 Main Male or 2 Main Female, lands on the tableau. We will pay extra attention to the direction of the seeker—the accuracy of your reading lies here. The picture below will help you understand the concept.

For a Male Querent

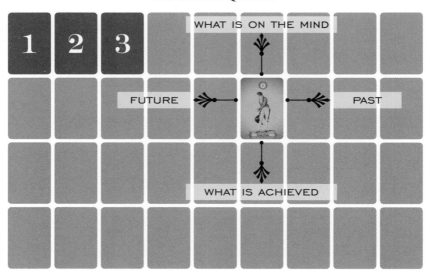

For a Female Querent

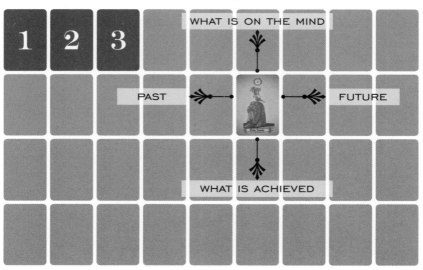

The position of the significator in the tableau gives valuable clues. If he/she is on the top row, this will indicate that he/she has control over the situation and knows how to deal with things. If he/she falls on the bottom row, this indicates that he/she has weight on his/her shoulders, the whole tableau is on top of him/her. Oftentimes, it's a sign that the querent is overwhelmed and has lost control on the course of events.

When the 1 Main Male happens to be in the first column on the left, this tells me that he is starting a new chapter of his life and looks forward to his future. Inversely, if he lands in the last column on the right, this tells me that he is at the end of a chapter and may be still attached to his past.

For a Female Querent

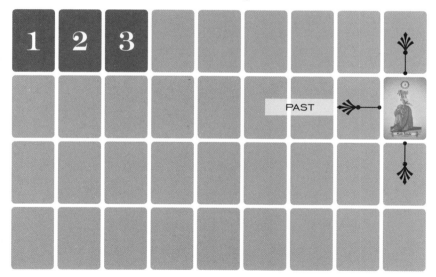

For a Male Querent

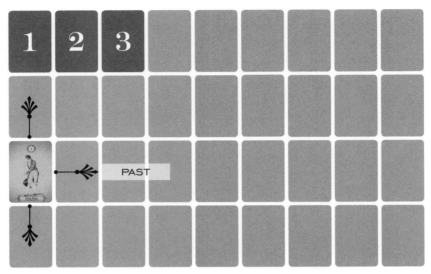

If the 2 Main Female is in the first column on the left, this announces the end of a chapter, and she is still attached to her past. Being in the last column on the right tells me that she is starting a new chapter of her life and looks forward to her future.

Many readers get panicked when this happens, as there are no cards showing the future of the querent; some will redeal or use another divination system to see the future. For my part, I never redeal the cards if the tableau appeared this way; it is for a reason. It's simply that a lesson needs to be learned before a future can happen.

You have already heard me say that a reading is always empowering rather than fatalistic, and you can't get blanks in a reading. Everything you hear, feel, notice, and sense is part of the reading—don't ever forget that. We are powerful, intuitive creatures, and the cards are just an extension of this psyche. Trust yourself more; this is what makes a good reader.

Key 3
THE FOUR CORNERS

I use the four corners of the tableau to see what the energy in action is and the dynamics; oftentimes these are things that the querent is not aware of. These can be elements that frame the situation; see it as pieces of tape that hold a poster or a large calendar in place on the wall. At this stage of the analysis, you should already have a sense of where the reading is going and what areas are pinpointed. Below are some examples of card meeting for the corners, giving you a sense of what I've been discussing.

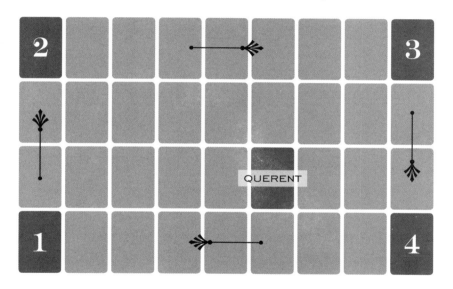

14 Sad News + 36 Hope, Big Water + 3 Marriage + 21 The Living Room

Indicates that some troubles happen in a relationship and that the querent still hopes to have some private time to solve the problem.

1 Main Male + 18 Small Child + 15 Success in Love + 7 A Pleasant Letter

Shows that the querent has started a new relationship and that communication between the couple is pleasant.

35 A Long Road + 9 A Change + 19 A Funeral + 17 A Gift

Announces a sign, a message from your loved ones in heaven, or the awakening of the querent's spiritual gifts.

32 Grief and Sorrow + 24 The Thievery + 6 The Good Lady +
8 False Person

A manipulative older woman is causing trouble; she may have taken away a precious ally from the querent.

23 The Court + 2 Main Female + 28 Expectation + 30 Legal Matters

The querent is in a court case and is expecting her lawyer to solve the situation. The querent may be in trial with a middle-aged woman, and a lawyer has to intervene.

11 Lot of Money + 33 Murky Thoughts + 25 High Honours +
27 Unexpected Money

Recognition and reward places the querent into a state of stress, not believing what is happening.

12 A Rich Girl + 4 A Meeting + 20 The House + 5 The Good Lord

If the reading is for a woman, the four corners are predicting an encounter with an older male, most likely during a family party. If the reading is for a man, he will meet a younger female at a family party.

Key 4
BOXING THE SIGNIFICATOR

This is where the 9-card spread or Box Spread becomes handy. You will box the significator and read the spread as explained previously in the chapter about the card spreads.

QUERENT

Key 5

THE KIPPER HOUSES

What are the Kipper Houses? The Kipper Houses are all of the 36 cards of the deck put in numerical order from 1 to 36, in a 9 × 4 formation.

The Kipper House

1	2	3	4	5	6	7	8	9
10	11	12	13	14	15	16	17	18
19	20	21	22	23	24	25	26	27
28	29	30	31	32	33	34	35	36

The houses are stagnant and never change, and each card that falls on them is colored by the energy of the house. For example, 17 A Gift in the house of the 7 A Pleasant Letter announces surprising positive news or a pleasant gift. I tend to see the houses as the space a card occupies: the 1 Main Male falling in the house of 25 High Honours would mean that the querent is busy with his studies, whereas the 2 Main Female falling in the house of 20 The House would be busy with domestic chores.

Let say the 2 Main Female is in the house of 3 Marriage. This will indicate that the female querent is in a serious partnership, or even being proposed to.

The house technique does add more dimension to the reading of the Grand Tableau. Pay attention to which house your significator falls on; this is precious information and can add details to your reading. When a card falls on its own house, the meaning is stronger; for instance, 29 The Prison in the house of 29 The Prison would mean a strong blockage, a mighty enemy.

Key 6
THE KNIGHTING

The knighting technique gives additional information on a card; the move is similar to the one in a chess game. The knight on the chessboard moves outward from a position in a perpendicular movement (L-shaped move). The original card of departure is then combined with the knighted cards. (See the diagram to help you visualize the move. S = Significator.)

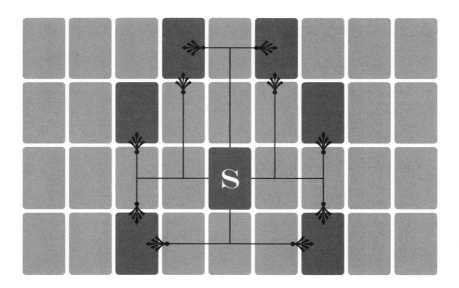

    For the knighting you can get more information on a particular situation by using the knighting method, starting with the card that stands as a significator to the situation; for instance, I want to know more on a family matter. I will use the knighting from The House card, as it represents family. For work I will use the Occupation card and so on. The knighting can be used on any card you want. Depending on the position of your significator in the tableau, you will get 2–8 knighted cards.

THE MIRRORING

This is a wonderful technique to use if you feel that your tableau is lacking information; please don't mirror every single card of the tableau, as this will bring confusion instead of clear information. The mirroring is the reflection of a card to its position in a spread. Start by picking a card that covers your topic, notice its position, and look at the card that has the same inverted position. The diagrams will help describe the technique.

We are paying attention here to card A, which is in the third row of the third column (from top to bottom), to get the mirroring card. Let's now first fold the GT in half vertically, and then half horizontally.

Here's what we get when we fold the GT in half vertically: position A is our significator or key card and position M is the mirroring card. Combine the mirrored pair together and read.

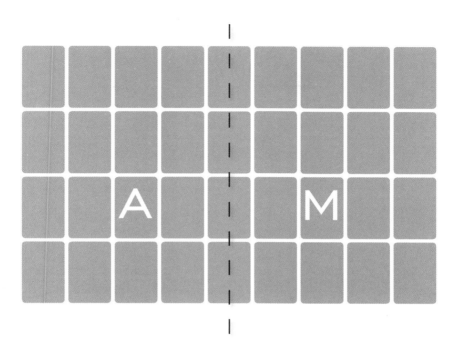

Then we fold the GT in half horizontally:

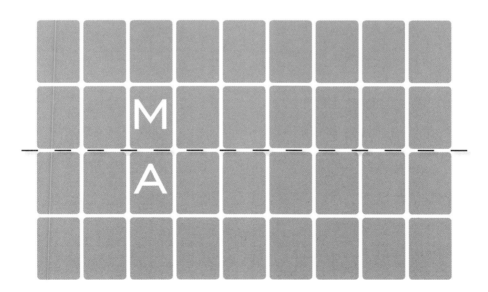

Again, we read the mirrored paired together, then read the trio:

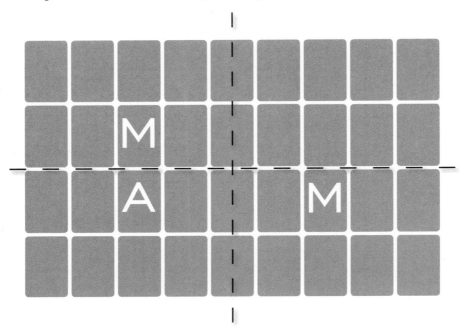

The mirroring provides 2–4 card combinations. What I love about this technique is that it will reveal things that people want to hide or an established pattern that perhaps the seeker is not aware of.

THE GRAND

TABLEAU

IN ACTION

$\mathcal{I}$ want to share with you a Grand Tableau I've cast for Marie-Eve. She is a repeat client of mine and trusts my readings. Her concern today was about her relationship with Hugues. They've live together for now more than fifteen years and have two children, a boy and a girl.

For a few months now, their relationship has started to degrade. Marie-Eve didn't know what to do and wanted the reading to shed light on her uncertainties. As I shuffled my cards, I asked her to think and to speak her questions out loud while she cut the deck. I always let my clients touch my cards; I want them to infuse their question into the cards and be involved in the process, explaining in the most clear fashion possible what messages the cards want to convey. (In the last chapter I will share with you my method of clearing and charging my cards; this will ensure the clarity of your reading, and you will no longer be afraid to let people touch your cards.)

I activated these four cards for the reading:

12 A Rich Girl: to represent her daughter

13 A Rich Man: to represent her son

1 Main Male: for the husband

3 Marriage: their relationship

The Grand Tableau will give the big picture of what is going on around the house, with the kids, with their intimacy, family, etc. Following you will find Marie-Eve's Grand Tableau.

We start with the first three cards of the tableau; remember these cards give the first note to the reading. See what is brought to the table. We have the 1 Main Man + 18 Small Child + 15 Success in Love. This combination of cards tells me that the husband is in charge; he is on the top of the tableau in his own house, making him the regent of the tableau. He is turning his back to both love and child—not the best start for the reading and for Marie-Eve.

Let's have a close look to the four corners of the tableau. This would add more details to what has already been said. I like to compare the Grand Tableau to an onion: as we peel through each layer, we get additional information till we hit the core.

Let's have a look at the four corners in the diagram:

1 Main Male

2 Main Female

28 Expectation

22 A Military

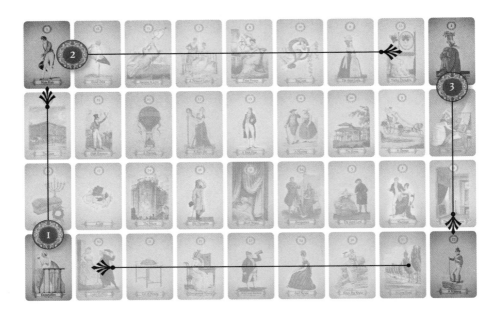

The energy is directly impacting Marie-Eve, as she is part of the corners. The cards clearly show that the 1 Main Male dominates the tableau; they are in a disharmonious relationship as their backs are turned to each other. They both have divergent expectations—Hugues is rude with Marie-Eve, and she in return defends herself, expecting Hugues to understand. But Hugues expects Marie-Eve to understand his point of view. What a headache!

At this point we have precise, clear, and valuable information on our seekers. There's more to come; let's continue with identifying the 2 Main Female.

The 2 Main Female is at the very end of the tableau; we see that in her past, she had a lot of joyful moments with motherhood, with a loving relationship, and with a comfortable financial situation.

Actually, there are no cards representing her future. This is because she is at the end of a chapter, and she has not yet made a decision about it. I suspect Marie-Eve to be involved in an affair—24 The Thievery + 21 The Living Room + 22 A Military shows me that clearly. No. 22 A Military can stand for another man in some readings.

The querent can't be boxed in a 9-card spread as there are not enough cards around her to box. Let's proceed to the House method.

Marie-Eve is in the House of 9 A Change relevant to her actual situation; she is in a big transition—perhaps even leaving her home. The other man shown here by 22 A Military is thinking of the cheating and the intimate time they had together (22 A Military + 21 The Living Room + 24 The Thievery + 2 Main Female). I use now the mirroring method, and the 2 Main Female mirrors 22 A Military, again showing proof that she is hiding something or someone that the GT reveals.

Let's take a look at her relationship with her husband. We are looking now at the 3 Marriage card, one that we had activated at the beginning of the reading.

I will use the Box Spread here to see where their relationship is heading. The 3 Marriage card sits in the house of 26 Big Luck, telling me that this relationship was an amazing one, a blessing for both partners. In the past (20 The House + 5 The Good Lord + 36 Hope, Big Water)

everything was fine; the man was caring, and they were kind to each other. In the present, both of them are thinking of moving away, of taking distance (9 A Change + 3 Marriage + 35 A Long Road). The future of their relationship is a lie; the woman is cheating with another man, perhaps someone who wears a uniform. The suspicion I got at the beginning of the reading, of their relationship coming to an end, is being confirmed.

Before ending the reading, I wanted to see how the kids were going to react to the situation. I've activated the 12 A Rich Girl and 13 A Rich Man to symbolize Marie-Eve's children.

The two cards face each other, showing that both are comforting one another. The boy is in the house of 14 Sad News—this situation really affects him. His hope is that this sad news turns into great news and that mommy and daddy continue to love each other. Sometimes readings can be very emotional, particularly where children are involved, like here.

The daughter, inversely, sees the manipulation, the lies, and the deception, and she knows that things will not get better.

I use the knighting technique for the boy, as I feel he is the one who is the more concerned by the situation, and I want the tableau to give me some practical advice for him. A lot of kids see their world falling apart when their parents separate; this often affects them on a high level.

The knighting shows that the kids can count on the grandparents to hold their hands during this hard time!

To punctuate the reading, I paid attention to the first and last cards; they are for me like the first and last pages of a storybook, card 36 being the punctuation. Here it is 22 A Military—the other man wins.

I must say that this was a reading with lots of emotion. As a reader, we are sensitive ones. Like a satellite dish we receive the transmission of energy; we feel the emotion of our clients and those concerned by the reading, and children are open vessels with their energy easy to access. Their sincerity and purity are amazing and often remind me of how I was when I was little, and I'm sure it's the same for you.

KIPPER

CORRESPONDENCES

LENORMAND

For those who already read the Lenormand oracle, Kipper card reading will be easier. The two systems are very close, and both decks have similar cards. The table lists the correspondence for both decks. It will be handy in case you don't understand a Kipper card; you could at that time compare it to its equivalence in the Lenormand.

LENORMAND	KIPPER
Rider	13 A Rich Man, 10 A Journey
Clover	27 Unexpected Money
Ship	35 A Long Way, 10 A Journey, 9 A Change
House	21 The Living Room
Tree	31 Short Illness
Clouds	33 Murky Thoughts
Snake	8 False Person
Coffin	32 Grief And Sorrow
Bouquet	17 A Gift, 12 A Rich Girl
Scythe	19 A Funeral
Whip	32 Grief and Sorrow
Birds	7 A Pleasant Letter
Child	18 Small Child
Fox	34 Occupation
Bear	34 Occupation, 5 The Good Lord
Stars	25 High Honours
Stork	18 Small Child, 9 A Change, 6 The Good Lady
Dog	13 A Rich Man
Tower	30 Legal Matters, 23 The Court, 29 The Prison, 22 A Military
Garden	4 A Meeting
Mountain	35 A Long Road, 29 The Prison
Crossroad	35 A Long Road
Mice	31 Short Illness, 24 The Thievery
Heart	15 Success in Love
Ring	3 Marriage
Book	33 Murky Thoughts
Letter	7 A Pleasant Letter
Man	1 Main Male
Woman	2 Main Female
Lilies	5 The Good Lord, 6 The Good Lady
Sun	26 Big Luck, 11 Lot of Money
Moon	25 High Honours
Key	26 Big Luck, 36 Hope, Big Water
Fish	34 Occupation, 11 Lot of Money
Anchor	28 Expectation
Cross	32 Grief And Sorrow

When you begin to read with the Kipper, everything starts with learning the meaning of the 36 cards. This can be quite frustrating for some of us; you are afraid of forgetting the key words and go blank during a reading. But don't worry; I am here to help you. Just relax and follow the memorization methods I am going to share with you right now.

UNDERSTANDING
THE MATERIAL

Take time to read your cards' meanings in a quiet place. Your brain will start to process the information, and reading aloud will greatly help.

REFLECT ON
YOUR MATERIAL

Once you've read the material, think about what it really means—instead of just reciting and learning by heart, you should understand the purpose behind the lines. For instance, understand the motivation of the 8 False Person; this will help you get a better sense of what this card means and how it can relate to a particular situation.

WRITE DOWN
THE MEANING

Once you've read and reflect on your material, write down the meaning. You can simplify and write what you've understood in your own words. Focusing on your writing will help your brain absorb everything you've learned.

3

MISTAKES

TO AVOID

WHEN READING KIPPER

3 Mistakes to Avoid When Reading Kipper

Mistake 1
"TAROTIZING" KIPPER

The Kipper oracle uses a language of its own. Don't ever read them like you would read the Tarot—they are two distinctive systems, and their approaches are different.

Mistake 2
SAME QUESTION AGAIN AND AGAIN

Beginners to Kipper sometimes tend to ask the same question more than once—over and over. They are unsure about the reply and think that the deck may be misinterpreting their question. When your reading feels uncertain and muddy, go back to your question. Remember: clear question equals clear answer! Sometimes your head may think about a question, but your mouth spills it out in another way. It's a good idea to note your question on paper in front of you and read it as you shuffle your cards.

Mistake 3
TO KEEP DRAWING EXTRA CARDS AS CLARIFIERS

Sometimes an extra card is needed to clarify a spread. The extra card will shed light on the reading. Often, newbies tend to draw clarifying cards until they finally see something they like—this is cheating with yourself! Stick to only one card as clarifier, and your reading will stay clear, honest, and accurate.

CLEARING AND

KIPPER CARDS

BLESSING YOUR

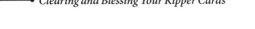
CLEARING YOUR KIPPER DECK

Oracle cards are sensitive, and because they absorb energy, you need to clear them before each reading you intend to conduct. Clearing the cards on a regular basis is essential since you don't want the energy of the previous person or reading to influence the new one you intend to give. When you clear the deck, you bring it back to its neutral state. There are many ways of clearing your cards; all are effective, but not all will work for you. I will explain some of the techniques I use, and hopefully this will inspire you to create your own ritual. Choose one that feels right and suits your needs and beliefs. Also note: Not only do the cards need to be cleared, but the box, pouch, or any item you house your deck in needs to be purified.

SETTING YOUR INTENTION THROUGH PRAYER

Always tell the cards what you would like them to do for you! They are your best friend. They listen and hear you, and the wisdom they convey is unlimited. You just need to ask. I believe in the power of prayer; prayer needs to belong to any religion and does not have to have any structured ways. For me, prayer is a heart-to-heart conversation with the most High, and you can ask whatever help you would like from your cards in your reading. When I clear my cards I often say:

> Dear God and all of my Spirit Guides and Angels, I ask that everything that is not from your Divine light be lifted away now from these cards. Thank you.

BLESSING YOUR CARDS

I use prayer to bless my cards. I speak an invocation as I hold them in my hands:

> Dear God, Spirit Guides, and Angels, I ask that these cards becomes a sacred tool for divine guidance and be a blessing for myself, my clients, and everyone involved. Help me stay centered so I may easily understand the messages that the cards want to convey. Thank you.

You can light a white or red candle next to your cards as a sign of blessing or expose them to moonlight. There are various ways you can bless your cards, and I always choose the simplest and shortest, as I found them to be more effective.

CRYSTALS AND SMUDGING

I also use crystals to clear my cards: angelite, lapis lazuli, celestine, selenite, and clear crystal quartz. I simply place one of them on top of my cards and let them sit for a few hours.

Smudging your cards with incense or white sage is a good way as well to clear and bless your Kipper deck; the smoke will banish any old energy from your cards and leave them fresh and clear.

My Daily Kipper Card Draw

Date _____

Question _____
_____

Guidance _____
_____
_____
_____
_____
_____
_____
_____
_____
_____

Notes —

My Daily Kipper Card Draw

Date _____

Question _____
_____

Guidance _____
_____
_____
_____
_____
_____
_____
_____
_____
_____
_____

Notes —

My Daily Kipper Card Draw

Date _____

Question _____

_____

Guidance _____

_____

_____

_____

_____

_____

_____

_____

_____

_____

Notes —

My Daily Kipper Card Draw

Date _____

Question _____

Guidance _____
_____
_____
_____
_____
_____
_____
_____
_____
_____

Notes —

My Daily Kipper Card Draw

Date _____

Question _____
_____

Guidance _____
_____
_____
_____
_____
_____
_____
_____
_____
_____

Notes —

My Daily Kipper Card Draw

Date _____

Question _____

_____

Guidance _____

_____

_____

_____

_____

_____

_____

_____

_____

_____

Notes —

My Daily Kipper Card Draw

Date _____

Question _____
_____

Guidance _____
_____
_____
_____
_____
_____
_____
_____
_____
_____

Notes —

My Daily Kipper Card Draw

Date _____

Question _____
_____

Guidance _____
_____
_____
_____
_____
_____
_____
_____
_____
_____
_____

Notes —

My Daily Kipper Card Draw

Date _____

Question _____

_____

Guidance _____

_____

_____

_____

_____

_____

_____

_____

_____

_____

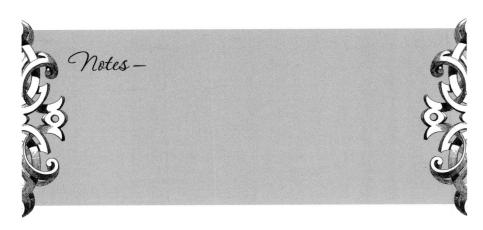

Notes —

My Daily Kipper Card Draw

Date _____

Question _____
_____

Guidance _____
_____
_____
_____
_____
_____
_____
_____
_____
_____
_____

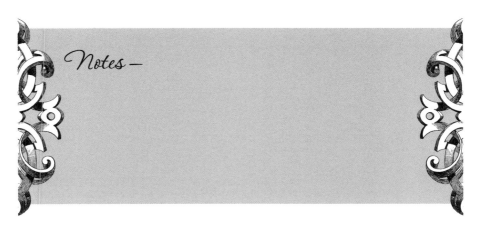

Notes —

My Daily Kipper Card Draw

Date _____

Question _____
_____

Guidance _____
_____
_____
_____
_____
_____
_____
_____
_____
_____

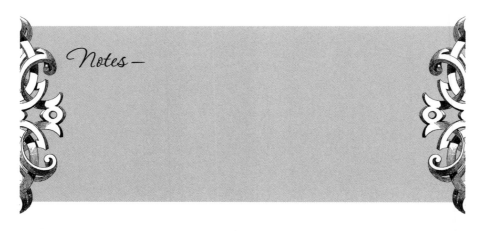

Notes —

My Daily Kipper Card Draw

Date _____

Question _____
_____

Guidance _____
_____
_____
_____
_____
_____
_____
_____
_____
_____

Notes —

My Daily Kipper Card Draw

Date _____

Question _____
_____

Guidance _____
_____
_____
_____
_____
_____
_____
_____
_____
_____
_____

Notes —

My Daily Kipper Card Draw

Date _____

Question _____
_____

Guidance _____
_____
_____
_____
_____
_____
_____
_____
_____
_____
_____

Notes —

My Daily Kipper Card Draw

Date _____

Question _____
_____

Guidance _____
_____
_____
_____
_____
_____
_____
_____
_____
_____

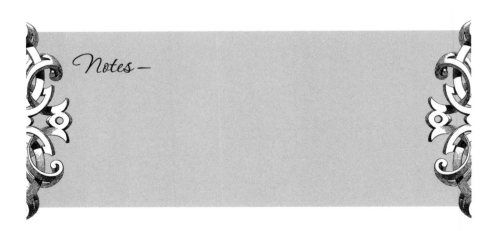

Notes —

My Daily Kipper Card Draw

Date _____

Question _____

_____

Guidance _____

_____

_____

_____

_____

_____

_____

_____

_____

_____

Notes —

My Daily Kipper Card Draw

Date _____

Question _____
_____

Guidance _____
_____
_____
_____
_____
_____
_____
_____
_____
_____

Notes —

My Daily Kipper Card Draw

Date _____

Question _____

_____

Guidance _____

_____

_____

_____

_____

_____

_____

_____

_____

_____

Notes —

My Daily Kipper Card Draw

Date _____

Question _____
_____

Guidance _____
_____
_____
_____
_____
_____
_____
_____
_____
_____
_____

Notes —

My Daily Kipper Card Draw

Date _____

Question _____

_____

Guidance _____

_____

_____

_____

_____

_____

_____

_____

_____

_____

Notes —

My Daily Kipper Card Draw

Date _____

Question _____
_____

Guidance _____
_____
_____
_____
_____
_____
_____
_____
_____
_____

Notes —

My Daily Kipper Card Draw

Date _____

Question _____

_____

Guidance _____

_____

_____

_____

_____

_____

_____

_____

_____

_____

Notes —

My Daily Kipper Card Draw

Date _____

Question _____
_____

Guidance _____
_____
_____
_____
_____
_____
_____
_____
_____
_____

Notes —

My Daily Kipper Card Draw

Date _____

Question _____

_____

Guidance _____

_____

_____

_____

_____

_____

_____

_____

_____

_____

Notes —

My Daily Kipper Card Draw

Date _____

Question _____
_____

Guidance _____
_____
_____
_____
_____
_____
_____
_____
_____
_____

Notes —

My Daily Kipper Card Draw

Date _____

Question _____
_____

Guidance _____
_____
_____
_____
_____
_____
_____
_____
_____
_____

Notes —

My Daily Kipper Card Draw

Date _____

Question _____
_____

Guidance _____
_____
_____
_____
_____
_____
_____
_____
_____
_____
_____

Notes —

My Daily Kipper Card Draw

Date _____

Question _____
_____

Guidance _____
_____
_____
_____
_____
_____
_____
_____
_____
_____
_____

Notes —

My Daily Kipper Card Draw

Date _____

Question _____
_____

Guidance _____
_____
_____
_____
_____
_____
_____
_____
_____
_____

Notes —

284

My Daily Kipper Card Draw

Date _____

Question _____
_____

Guidance _____
_____
_____
_____
_____
_____
_____
_____
_____
_____

Notes —

My Daily Kipper Card Draw

Date _____

Question _____

_____

Guidance _____

_____

_____

_____

_____

_____

_____

_____

_____

_____

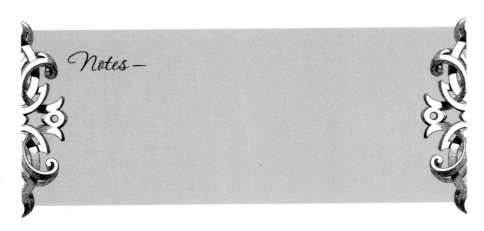

Notes —

My Daily Kipper Card Draw

Date _____

Question _____
_____

Guidance _____
_____
_____
_____
_____
_____
_____
_____
_____
_____
_____

Notes —

ACKNOWLEDGMENTS

I have to start by thanking all my students and followers around the world; you infused the idea of this book in my mind. I am so honored to be the first author to have written an English book on Kipper. *None of this would have been possible without you.*

To dear friends and my family, who stood by my side and encouraged my ideas and aspirations. To my wife, Erika, for her fourteen years of patience and understanding; you are my soulmate, and I am so grateful to have you in my life—I love you. To my two little monsters, Raphaël and Mathilde, who don't make my task of writing easy, but I can't think of life without you; you are sunshine and I love you so much.

To all the people who have given me the chance to read the stories of their lives with my cards; I am the one blessed in these encounters. I've learned so much through you.

To my followers on social media, especially my YouTube subscribers: you are awesome. Our tribe is constantly growing; thank so much for your support.

To Schiffer Publishing, for giving me the chance to share my art with the world and believing in my Kipper skills.

Last but not least, to my Angels, Spirit Guides, and Ancestors; thank you so much for blessing, listening, and being open to me. Your guidance made my life so easy.

Merci, Merci, Merci